AIR CAMPAIGN

SOUTH ATLANTIC 1982

The carrier campaign in the Falklands War

ANGUS KONSTAM | ILLUSTRATED BY EDOUARD A. GROULT

OSPREY PUBLISHING
Bloomsbury Publishing Plc
Kemp House, Chawley Park, Cumnor Hill, Oxford OX2 9PH, UK
29 Earlsfort Terrace, Dublin 2, Ireland
1385 Broadway, 5th Floor, New York, NY 10018, USA
E-mail: info@ospreypublishing.com
www.ospreypublishing.com

OSPREY is a trademark of Osprey Publishing Ltd

First published in Great Britain in 2025

© Osprey Publishing Ltd, 2025

All rights reserved. No part of this publication may be reproduced or transmitted in any form or by any means, electronic or mechanical, including photocopying, recording, or any information storage or retrieval system, without prior permission in writing from the publishers.

A catalogue record for this book is available from the British Library.

ISBN: PB 9781472864710; eBook 9781472864727;
ePDF 9781472864697; XML 9781472864703

25 26 27 28 29 10 9 8 7 6 5 4 3 2 1

Maps and diagrams by www.bounford.com
3D BEVs by Paul Kime
Index by Zoe Ross
Typeset by PDQ Digital Media Solutions, Bungay, UK
Printed by Repro India Ltd.

Title page: If any one weapon of war came to symbolize the Falklands Conflict it was the British Aerospace Sea Harrier, a small, nimble vertical short take-off and landing (V/STOL) jet fighter, which fulfilled the Royal Navy's need for fixed wing aviation, at a time when the fleet had been stripped of its last large carriers.

Osprey Publishing supports the Woodland Trust, the UK's leading woodland conservation charity.

To find out more about our authors and books visit www.ospreypublishing.com. Here you will find extracts, author interviews, details of forthcoming events and the option to sign up for our newsletter.

Author's Note
I have retained imperial measurements for Argentinian armament as is their protocol.
All ranks are in English for consistency purposes.
All photos courtesy of the Stratford Archive.

Argentinian and British rank equivalents			
Argentinian Fuerza Aérea	Argentinian Armada	British Royal Air Force	British Royal Navy
Comodoro	Capitán de navao	Group Captain	Captain
Vicecomodoro	Capitán de Fregata	Wing Commander	Commander
Mayor	Capitán de Corbeta	Squadron Leader	Lieutenant Commander
Capitán	Teniente de navao	–	Lieutenant
Primer teniente	Teniente de fragata	Flight Lieutenant	Sub-Lieutenant
Teniente	Teniente de corbeta	Flying Officer	–
Alférez	Guardia-marina	Pilot Officer	Midshipman

– no equivalent rank

AIR CAMPAIGN

CONTENTS

INTRODUCTION	4
CHRONOLOGY	6
ATTACKER'S CAPABILITIES	8
DEFENDER'S CAPABILITIES	13
CAMPAIGN OBJECTIVES	22
THE CAMPAIGN	31
ANALYSIS AND CONCLUSION	92
FURTHER READING	94
INDEX	95

INTRODUCTION

The Sea Harrier, affectionately known as the 'SHAR', after its usual description in official logs, status boards and paperwork. This plane, '001', was aircraft XZ493 embarked in HMS *Invincible*, which flew 35 sorties during the conflict. The SHAR's usual pilot during this period was Flt Lt Ian Mortimer.

On the morning of Friday 2 April 1982, Argentinian troops invaded the Falklands Islands, a British Overseas Territory in the South Atlantic, 300 miles from the coast of South America. By the end of the day the archipelago's capital, Port Stanley, was under Argentinian military occupation. When reports of the invasion reached London, almost 8,000 miles away, after consulting with senior military figures, the Prime Minister and her Cabinet decided to respond with force. The British Admiralty was duly ordered to dispatch a naval Task Force, to recapture the Falkland Islands. Three days later, on Monday 5 April, this hastily assembled Task Force sailed from Portsmouth.

The Task Force, commanded by Rear Admiral Sandy Woodward, was centred around a Carrier Battle Group (CVBG), made up of the aircraft carriers *Hermes* and *Invincible*. Each of them had Sea Harrier fighter jets and Sea King helicopters embarked. Other forces joined the Task Force as it steamed south, including a Commando brigade, more escorts and supply vessels, and hastily commandeered transports. Despite a UN resolution calling for the Argentinians to withdraw, diplomatic efforts failed, and the Task Force continued south towards the Falklands.

Many military analysts considered success impossible. The islands could only be liberated following an amphibious landing, supported by the aircraft and warships of the Task Force. Its success largely depended on controlling the skies over the beachhead, and the large disparity in the number of available aircraft suggested this was unlikely. The British had 42 jet fighters embarked in the Task Force, two-thirds of them Fleet Air Arm Sea Harriers, and the rest hastily converted Royal Air Force Harrier GR3s. This was roughly a third of the jet fighters available to the Argentine Air Force. Still, British pilots were confident in the capabilities of their aircraft, and in their own professionalism.

It was late May before the naval air war began in earnest, as Operation *Sutton* began – the landing of British troops at San Carlos Bay in East Falkland. Inevitably, the amphibious force and its naval escorts were subjected to sustained air attacks as they lay in this confined anchorage. So, it was up to the British Harriers to protect the landing operation, as well as

their own carrier battle group. Ultimately, they were highly successful in this air battle over the Falklands, despite the loss of three British warships in San Carlos, and another at sea, where it was screening the carriers.

It soon became evident that the Harrier had the edge over its Argentinian rivals. The small British jets were far more manoeuvrable than their opponents, and proved greatly superior in an aerial dogfight. By the time a ceasefire was declared on 14 June, these Fleet Air Arm and RAF Harriers had shot down 21 Argentine jets, while 18 more were destroyed by the Task Force's air defences. By contrast only two Sea Harriers and three Harrier GR3s were shot down by ground fire. None of them were lost in aerial combat. The Harrier jet proved to be the real star of the Falklands War.

The air campaign over the Falklands was a real test under fire, which showed the way forward in terms of naval aviation and fleet air defence for decades to come. This, then, is the story of how the air campaign played out and explains why the Harrier proved such a success.

The British Aerospace Sea Harrier FRS.1 was the latest embodiment of the design of a vertical take-off and landing (V/STOL) aircraft which first began in the 1960s. Trials were conducted, but it was 1975 before they were adopted by the Royal Navy, following the scrapping of carriers capable of operating larger fixed-wing aircraft.

CHRONOLOGY

April

2 April Argentinian troops invade the Falkland Islands and occupy Port Stanley.

3 April UN Security Council Resolution 502 passed.

5 April A British Task Force sails from Portsmouth, spearheaded by a carrier battle group.

9 April Most of 3 Cdo Bde heads south to join the task force.

12 April Maritime Exclusion Zone imposed around Falkland Islands by British government.

19 April Carrier battle group enters South Atlantic.

20–25 April Operation *Paraquet* – successful recapture of South Georgia from Argentinians.

30 April 200 n. mile Total Exclusion Zone (TEZ) enforced around Falkland Islands.

May

1 May Task Force launches first attacks on Falklands – Port Stanley airfield attacked; Operation *Black Buck* – RAF Vulcan raid on Port Stanley airfield.

2 May Argentinian cruiser *General Belgrano* torpedoed and sunk by submarine HMS *Conqueror*; Exocet attack by Super Étendards and air strike from Argentinian carrier both aborted.

4 May Destroyer HMS *Sheffield* attacked by Exocet to south-east of Falklands; second RAF *Black Buck* raid on Port Stanley airfield; Sea Harrier lost to ground fire over Goose Green.

6 May Two Sea Harriers lost to south-east of Falklands – suspected mid-air collision.

7 May TEZ extended to within 12 miles of Argentinian coast.

9 May Two Argentinian Skyhawks shot down over South Jason Island.

10 May Bad weather limits flying operations; *Sheffield* finally sinks after attempts to tow her fail; major reinforcements leave UK, including the liner *QE2*, serving as troopship.

12 May Four Argentinian Skyhawks shot down.

11–15 May SAS conduct Pebble Island raid. *Hermes* provides air cover.

17–18 May Special Forces land on Argentinian coast. *Invincible* provides air cover.

20 May Carrier battle group stationed to east of Falklands, in preparation for Operation *Sutton*.

21 May Operation *Sutton* – British landings at San Carlos Bay in East Falkland; major air operations over San Carlos – Harrier GR3 lost, as well as 12 Argentinian aircraft; Frigate HMS *Ardent* mortally damaged – several other warships suffer minor damage.

22 May Harrier GR3s attack airstrips in Falklands.

23 May Frigate HMS *Antelope* damaged by unexploded bomb and sinks following day; Sea Harrier lost to north-east of Falklands; two Argentinian aircraft destroyed.

24 May Three Argentinian Daggers shot down by Sea Harriers over Pebble Island; four Argentinian Skyhawks shot down over San Carlos.

25 May (Argentinian National Day) HMS *Coventry* sunk by bombs off Pebble Island, after downing a Skyhawk; RFA *Atlantic Conveyor* sunk to north-east of Falklands.

26–28 May Land battle at Goose Green – settlement recaptured by British. Support provided by Harrier GR3s.

31 May 3 Cdo Bde attacks Top Malo House, East Falkland; *Black Buck* raid on Port Stanley airfield.

June

1 June Sea Harrier lost to SAM fire south of Port Stanley.

4 June Yomp by 3 Cdo Bde brings it within sight of Port Stanley; *Black Buck* raid on Port Stanley airfield.

8 June Argentinian Canberras bomb American-flagged tanker north of TEZ; frigate HMS *Plymouth* damaged by bomb and Harrier GR3 lost over San Carlos; landing ship RFA *Sir Galahad* badly damaged by bombs in Bluff Cove. Scuttled as war grave.

11–12 June Land battles for Mount Longdon, Two Sisters, Mount Harriet.

13–14 June Land battles for Wireless Ridge, Tumbledown Hill.

14 June Surrender of Argentinian forces around Port Stanley – ceasefire; warships from Task Force enter Port Stanley harbour.

July

4 July *Hermes* leaves Falklands, bound for UK.

21 July *Hermes* arrives in Portsmouth, greeted by cheering crowds.

28 July *Invincible* relieved off Falklands by carrier *Illustrious*.

September

17 September *Invincible*, the last of the Carrier Battle Group, arrives in Portsmouth.

During the campaign a number of Royal Air Force versions of the Harrier, the GR.3 of No. 1 (Fighter) Sqn., were sent to the South Atlantic to reinforce the British CVBG. Two of them can be seen here, easily spotted by their longer snout-like nose. They were primarily used for ground-attack missions.

ATTACKER'S CAPABILITIES
South Atlantic strike force

A Dassault Mirage III fighter of the Argentinian air force pictured during the conflict. These elderly French-built aircraft formed the Grupo 8 de Caza, based in Comodoro Rivadavia and Río Gallegos. However, after initial losses, and the first Vulcan strike of 1 May, they were withdrawn from the air campaign, to protect the Argentinian mainland from further Vulcan attacks.

In the spring of 1982 the Argentine Air Force (*Fuerza Aérea Argentina*, or FAA) was a fairly powerful force, equipped with modern jet aircraft, but it was not prepared for an air war against Britain. Since its inception 70 years before, the most likely opponent of the FAA was Chile. So, everything from its aircraft and equipment to planning, doctrine and training had been focused on preparation for a war with its neighbour to the west rather than one against a European maritime power in the South Atlantic. The decision by the Argentinian junta to invade the Falkland Islands came as a surprise to the FAA, and it had to rapidly develop an operational plan to support the Argentinian troops on the island, and the Argentine Navy's operations in the theatre. However well equipped the FAA was, this was a war for which it was ill-prepared.

In April 1982, the FAA had a strength of around 240 aircraft. Not all of these were modern jets though, and a sizeable number were stationed in airfields close to the Chilean border, rather than near the Atlantic seaboard. Due to an arms embargo by the United States, many of the FAA's American-built aircraft were in a poor state of repair. Another limitation was the ability to refuel while airborne. The FAA only possessed two refuelling tankers, and as extended operations over the Falklands required small-range aircraft like the A-4 Skyhawk to refuel, this limited the number of aircraft which could operate together on an extended mission. However, the FAA's aircraft still greatly outnumbered the aircraft embarked in the British Task Force, and so the Argentinians were able to undertake sustained air operations during the Falklands conflict and posed a considerable threat to the Royal Navy's Carrier Battle Group.

The command structure of the FAA was somewhat complicated. It was divided into a Strategic Air Command (*Comando Aéreo Estratégico*, or CAE), which coordinated offensive air units throughout Argentina, and an Air Defence Command (*Comando Aéreo de Defensa*, or CAD), which oversaw the radar network, surface-to-air missile (SAM) defences and high-speed jet interceptors. Both of these took their orders from Brigadier Lami Dozo of the FAA, and a member of President Leopoldo Galtieri's military junta, which governed the country. His headquarters was in the FAA headquarters building in Buenos Aires. The CAE was divided into regional areas, including the Southern Air Force (*Fuerza Aérea Sur*, or FAS). It was the main force involved in the air campaign over the Falklands. The FAS operated from the six military air bases in the Argentinian region of Patagonia. These were close to Argentina's Atlantic coast, and within range of the Falkland Islands. Its main strike aircraft were Mirage IIIs, Daggers, Canberras and Skyhawks, as well as small turboprop-powered Pucarás.

The Argentine Navy (*Armada de la República Argentina*, or ARA) also maintained its own small air wing, the *Comando de la Aviación Naval Argentina* (or COAN), which operated the A-4 Skyhawk jet aircraft embarked in the navy's aircraft carrier, the *Veinticinco de Mayo*. At the time, the COAN was in the midst of replacing these American-built strike aircraft with larger French-built Super Étendard strike aircraft. So, both types of aircraft were available, with the latter based ashore, together with some MB-338 light strike aircraft and T-34 Mentor prop-planes. These land-based aircraft fell within the control of Vice Admiral Juan Lombardo's South Atlantic Military Theatre (*Teatro Operaciones Atlántico Sur*), which assumed control of all naval operations in the South Atlantic, including the use of land-based naval strike aircraft, and naval air assets deployed in the Falkland Islands.

This overlapped slightly with the responsibilities of the Falklands Military Garrison (*Guarnición Militar Malvinas*), which had a small air component, under the command of an air force brigadier based at Port Stanley. All of these were prop planes: Pucarás, Mentors and MB-338s, or helicopters. Finally, the Argentine Army (*Ejército Argentino*, or EA) maintained a small air wing, which operated various helicopters. However, despite this assortment of commands and various service interests, for the most part air operations during the campaign were coordinated effectively by Brigadier Ernesto Crespo, commander of the Southern Air Force, who was based at Comodoro Rivadavia air force base, 480 miles north-west of Port Stanley. For the sake of effectiveness, he also commanded navy and army air assets within his theatre of operations.

Air Chief Marshal (*Brigadier General*) Basilio Lami Dozo, the 53-year-old commander-in-chief of the *Fuerza Aérea Argentina* (Argentinian Air Force), and a member of the military triumvirate which formed the country's ruling junta, while he was strategic head of the air campaign waged against the British Task Force.

Brigadier Crespo's aircraft were scattered between the six air bases on the Patagonian coast controlled by the Southern Air Force. From north to south these were: Trelew and Comodoro Rivadavia in Chubut province; Puerto San Julián, Santa Cruz and Río Gallegos in Santa Cruz province; and Río Grande in Tierra del Fuego. These were between 380 and 580 miles from Port Stanley, which greatly limited the time these land-based aircraft could spend over the Falklands archipelago. The closest of them was the southernmost: Río Grande air force base, 380 miles to the south-west of Port Stanley. Puerto San Julián and Santa Cruz were almost directly west of the archipelago, and 435–440 miles from Port Stanley.

For the most part active combat sorties would be carried out by three main types of strike aircraft. The first was the American-built Douglas A-4 Skyhawk. This small attack aircraft was first developed in the mid-1950s, and was used by the US Navy until 1976, and the US Marine Corps until 1985, when ironically it was replaced by the AV-8 Harrier. The Skyhawk entered service with the Argentine Air Force in the mid-1960s, and the navy in 1972. Five years later though, a US arms embargo led to the dearth of spare parts for these Argentinian Skyhawks. As a result, aircraft numbers dropped, as some were cannibalized to keep the remainder in service. Even these had problems, the most notable being the ejector seats, which didn't work. Still, 48 Skyhawks took part in the Falklands conflict, carrying conventional bombs. These proved highly effective, sinking the destroyer HMS *Coventry* and mortally damaging the frigate HMS *Antelope* and the landing ship RFA *Sir Galahad*. This made these old bomb-armed aircraft singularly effective. In all, 22 of these Skyhawks were lost during the conflict, eight of them at the hands of British Harriers.

The Israeli-built Dagger was a multi-role fighter, the export version of the Nesher, which in turn was the Israeli name for the Mirage 5, co-produced by the French firm Dassault and

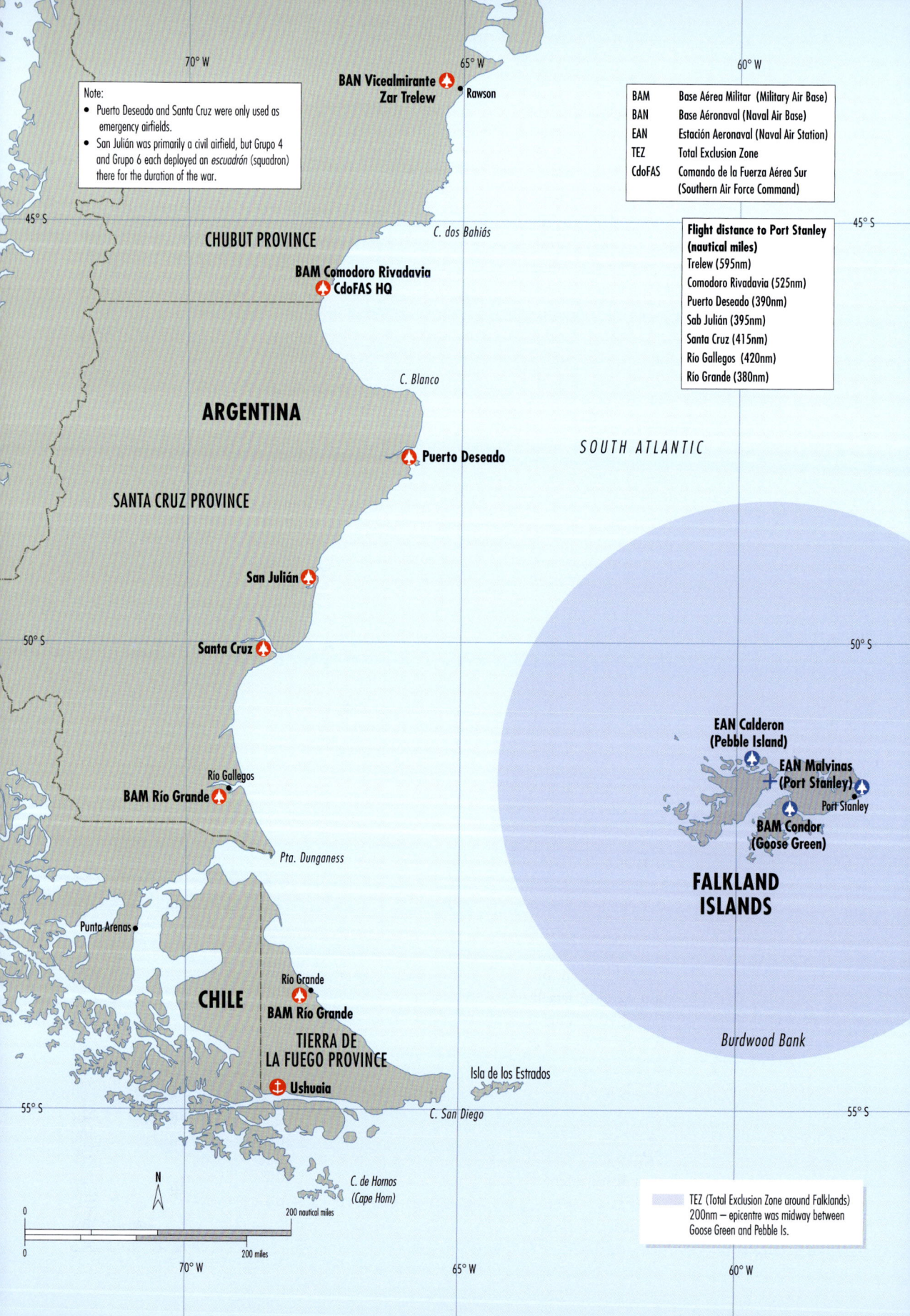

OPPOSITE ARGENTINIAN AIR BASES, 1982

the Israeli aircraft industry. The Dagger, Nesher and Mirage 5 were, in turn, an improved version of the older Dassault Mirage IIIC. In all, 153 sorties were conducted by the two Argentinian squadrons of Daggers during the Falklands conflict, and were responsible for damaging several Royal Navy warships, including the mortal blow that led to the loss of the frigate HMS *Ardent*. Their limitation, however, was a relatively low capability in terms of air combat. In total, 11 Daggers were shot down, all but two losses being at the hands of British Sea Harriers. Another two were lost due to mechanical failure. A major limiting factor of the Dagger was its lack of an air-to-air refuelling capability. This meant that these aircraft only had an 11-minute loiter time over San Carlos Water – a small enough window to locate a target, bomb it and then withdraw from the area, all the while under the threat of interception by British Harriers.

In the aftermath of the US arms embargo, the Argentine Navy turned to France, and ordered 14 Dassault-Breuget Super Étendard strike aircraft, and by 1982 four of the five of these in Argentina were operational and equipped with a single Exocet anti-ship missile. The AM-39 air-launched version of this French-built sea-skimming missile had an effective range of 38nm. The limitation, of course, was that the Argentinians only had four aircraft and five missiles – too few to pose a major threat to the British Task Force. Still, the Argentinian naval pilots gave it their best shot. These aircraft and their missiles were responsible for hits on the destroyer HMS *Sheffield* and the merchantman SS *Atlantic Conveyor*, which was carrying helicopters and supplies for use by British forces. Both ships subsequently sank.

The other substantial strike aircraft used by the FAA during the conflict was the British-designed Canberra, a jet-powered medium bomber, built in Britain, the United States and Australia, and first introduced in the early 1950s. The Canberra had a remarkably long life, was modified into several variants, and was exported widely. Argentina bought ten of the B.62 version in the early 1970s, a refurbished version of the British B.2 bomber. Six of these were still operational in 1982. During the conflict these Canberras operated from Trelew air force base, flying 54 sorties, most of which were bombing missions against the British Task Force. However, their efforts proved unsuccessful, and two Canberras were shot down, one by a ship's air defence missile, and the other in an attack by a Sea Harrier.

One of the main problems facing the FAA that spring was the lack of operational aircraft. The official strength of the air force was considerably greater than the number of available aircraft, as many had been mothballed due to a shortage of parts, lack of airworthiness or maintenance, or through obsolescence. So, although the FAA possessed 65 Skyhawks, only 46 of them were fully operational. Similarly, only six out of ten Canberras and 11 out of 16 Mirage fighters. An exception were the Israeli-built Daggers, with all 34 of them ready for service. In all, instead of 116 fighters and attack aircraft capable of operating over the Falklands, only 97 or so were available for operations. In fact, Brigadier Dozo placed the FAA's total at just 87.

In addition, there were the 11 Skyhawks and five Super Étendards operated by the Argentine Navy, of which one had recently been cannibalized for parts to keep the remaining four in operation. Also not included in this total were the smaller aircraft deployed in airfields within the occupied Falkland Islands. These amounted to another 34 Pucará or Turbo-Mentor propeller planes, and Macchi light attack jets, which had virtually no anti-aircraft or anti-ship capability. Their main role was to support the Argentinian garrison on the Falkland Islands. If these were added to the total, that gave the Argentinians around 130 operational

While Brigadier General Dozo made the strategic decisions concerning the air campaign, operational control was devolved to his subordinate, Air Vice-Marshal ('*Brigadier*') Ernesto Horacio Crespo, commander-in-chief of the *Comando de la Fuerza Aérea Sur* (CdoFAS, or Southern Air Force Command), based at BAM Comodoro Rivadavia.

aircraft available to them during the conflict. Even without the smaller aircraft in the theatre, this still gave the Argentinians a numerical superiority of around four to one in the campaign.

There were other factors that limited the effectiveness of the Argentine Air Force. The first was training. However skilled the pilots of the FAA and COAN might be, only the naval pilots were fully trained to attack ships at sea. Until the Falklands conflict demanded otherwise, the FAA had trained its own pilots and air crew to fight in a land-based campaign over South America, rather than over the South Atlantic. Then, while COAN's small cadre of Exocet-armed Super Étendards possessed the very latest in anti-ship weaponry, COAN's Skyhawk pilots, together with all FAA pilots, only had conventional World War II era 'iron bombs' available to them, rather than the latest generation of 'smart' munitions. For the most part, that meant American-manufactured bombs.

Exocet AM-39 anti-ship missile	
Dimensions	Length 19ft 8in (6m)
	Weight: 1,720lb (780kg)
Warhead	364lb (165kg)
Guidance	Infra active radar homing
Speed	620 knots (Mach 0.93)
Attitude	Sea-skimming
Launch Platform	Argentinian Super Étendard strike fighter

Some also had the capability to carry unguided rockets, although COAN also had a small number of light anti-ship missiles, designed for use against enemy patrol boats or surfaced submarines. So, given the lack of warning about the Falklands invasion, these FAA airmen had little time to learn the new skills needed to bomb naval targets instead of land ones. Essentially, COAN instructors had about two weeks to train these FAA bomber pilots, before they were called upon to carry out their first bombing sorties.

The range to the target has already been discussed – giving most pilots a very short time over the target before a lack of fuel forced them to return to base. This also limited their ability to manoeuvre if attacked by British Harriers during the return leg of their flight. The Argentinians only had two refuelling tankers capable of refuelling aircraft in mid-air. However, two FAA KC-130 Hercules transports were converted into additional fuelling aircraft, and these were attached to COAN's 2 Escuadrilla (*Squadron*), which was equipped with the five Super Étendards. Through April these navy pilots trained in mid-air refuelling, so when the time came to fly operational sorties, they at least were able to operate at extended ranges. The remaining two refuelling aircraft were simply too few to refuel squadron-sized formations while airborne. Also, only Canberras and Skyhawks were equipped for mid-air refuelling. So, this limited the size and composition of attacking formations during the conflict.

Despite the Argentinian superiority in numbers, their air force had its limitations. They relied on old planes, many of which had mechanical shortcomings, such as the non-functioning ejector seats in the Skyhawks. Many lacked modern air-search or surface-search radar, or the ability to carry air-to-air missiles. This made them vulnerable in air combat, and Argentinian losses during the conflict reflected that. When attacking naval targets, all but the five Super Étendards were forced to use conventional bombs, and most pilots lacked the specialist training needed to use them effectively. Only the Exocet missile was considered a modern anti-ship weapon. Despite all this, the Argentinian pilots carried out their attacks with commendable dedication, particularly during the attacks on the British amphibious landing in San Carlos Water. Their courage earned them the admiration of their opponents. It didn't, however, make up for their combination of inadequate training and poor equipment.

DEFENDER'S CAPABILITIES
Air power of the Task Force

The British response was to send a Task Force to recover the Falkland Islands. At its core would be a Carrier Battle Group, centred around two relatively small aircraft carriers, HMS *Hermes* and HMS *Invincible*. Creating this small force though, wasn't a straightforward task, especially given the speed with which the Task Force was assembled. Both carriers had just been involved in NATO exercises, with *Hermes* used as a Commando assault ship, and *Invincible* in her usual role as an anti-submarine carrier. Both were in Portsmouth, with their aircraft disembarked and the bulk of their crews either on leave or about to go. *Hermes* was also undergoing a maintenance period, so she was draped in scaffolding, and many of her mechanical and electrical systems were being overhauled.

On Thursday 1 April the crews of both carriers were recalled or their leave was cancelled, and the ships were put at 48 hours' notice for sea. This was in response to the Admiralty's warning that an Argentinian attack was considered likely. Capt Linley Middleton of *Hermes* and Capt Jeremy Black of *Invincible* then oversaw what would be a frenetic few days. Normally *Hermes* carried just five Sea Harriers from 800 Naval Air Squadron (NAS), together with 18 Sea King helicopters. *Invincible* also carried five Sea Harriers, which made up 801 NAS, and nine Sea King helicopters. For Operation *Corporate* – the name now given to the Falklands operation – both squadrons would be brought up to their assigned wartime strength of eight to 12 aircraft. Then, the two carriers would function primarily as platforms for the Sea Harrier, with helicopter operations relegated to a secondary role.

While the Task Force prepared for sea in Portsmouth, amid a scene of frenzied but organized activity, the aircraft were prepared for the operation at their shore base, the Royal Naval Air Station at Yeovilton in Somerset. The first eight of them from 800 NAS were flown to Portsmouth and landed on *Hermes* on 2 April, the day of the Argentinian invasion. Three more followed on Sunday 4 April, together with four more Sea Harriers from 801 NAS which were embarked in *Invincible*. One of the squadron's aircraft was unserviceable and remained under repair in Yeovilton.

As a V/STOL jet fighter the Sea Harrier could take off and land vertically, and hover in place, by redirecting its exhaust nozzles downwards. It was thought this would be a feature which would prove a benefit in a dogfight, but during the Falklands conflict the SHAR pilots never resorted to it, as their aircraft was already highly manoeuvrable.

OPPOSITE THE FALKLAND ISLANDS, 1982

To bring these squadrons up to their wartime strength, Sea Harriers were gathered from other outfits. For 800 NAS, three came from 899 NAS, which was a training squadron, two were reserve aircraft held in storage, and one was sent which was being used for experimental missile trials. In all, 20 Sea Harriers were gathered for the operation, the last one from 899 NAS embarking in *Hermes* in the English Channel, just after the Task Force sailed. Four more from 899 NAS joined the four from 801 NAS which embarked in *Invincible*, to bring the squadron up to its wartime strength of eight aircraft. Sea King helicopters were also embarked, to provide anti-submarine protection for the Task Force. The final tally was 12 Sea Harriers of 800 NAS embarked in *Hermes*, and eight aircraft of 801 NAS in *Invincible*.

These though, weren't enough. There was a shortage of suitably qualified Fleet Air Arm pilots. So, seven Royal Air Force (RAF) pilots were attached to the squadrons, all of whom had been trained in naval aviation. Some were flown in at the last minute from bases in West Germany. Also, two more RAF pilots were added to the group, who were still undergoing operational flying training in naval aviation. They though, would have to complete their course during the voyage south. As well as pilots, the Sea Harriers needed a team of mechanics too. So, the support team for both Fleet Air Arm squadrons was expanded, and embarked in the two carriers, together with equipment and spare parts. To achieve all this in a matter of days was nothing short of a miracle. It was only matched by the herculean effort to get the ships of the Task Force supplied, manned and brought to full operational readiness by 5 April.

The Sea Harrier was a truly remarkable aircraft. Given the numerical odds facing the British, it would have to be. Unlike the Daggers and Mirages that would face them, these

Aircraft armament	
AIM-9B Sidewinder (developed 1956) – mounted in Argentinian naval A-4Q Skyhawk	
Type	Rear-aspect IR homing AAM
Speed	Mach 1.7
Range	5.4nm (lock effective: 2.16nm)
AIM-9L Sidewinder (1977) – mounted in Royal Naval Sea Harrier	
Type	All-aspect IR/Laser homing AAM
Speed	Mach 2.5
Range	9.72nm (lock effective: 2.2nm if rear aspect, 5.94nm from all other aspects)
Shafrir-2 (1971) – mounted in Argentinian A-4B Skyhawk and Dagger	
Type	Rear-aspect IR homing AAM
Speed	Mach 1.7
Range	5.4nm (lock effective: 1.6nm)
Matra R530 (1975) – mounted in Argentinian Mirage III	
Type	Rear-aspect IR homing AAM
Speed	Mach 2.7
Range	9.72nm (lock effective: 5.94nm)
R.550 Magic 1 (1976) – mounted in Argentinian Mirage III	
Type	Rear-aspect IR or Semi Active Radar homing AAM
Speed	Mach 2
Range	5.4nm (lock effective 2.9nm)
1 nautical mile = 2,025yds (1,852m)	

were subsonic jets, with a maximum speed of 618 knots, or Mach 0.94, if flown at sea level. An Argentinian Dagger could fly at Mach 2.1, or just over twice the speed of the Sea Harrier. The Mirage IIIC was a little faster, with a top speed of Mach 2.1. However, although these had never been tested in combat, the Sea Harrier had, potentially, a couple of all-important advantages. The first was its armament. Like these two Argentinian jets, the Sea Harrier was armed with the Sidewinder air-to-air missile (AAM). However, while the Argentinians used the AIM-9B version, which had been in use during the Vietnam War, the Sea Harrier carried the AIM-9l (or 'Lima' version), first introduced in 1977.

Both were heat-seeking missiles, with an effective range of about 2–3 miles, and a speed of Mach 2.5. However, unlike the older Argentinian version, which could only home in on the rear aspect of a target, the 'Lima' was an 'all-aspect' missile and could be launched from just about any angle, and even had a potential ability to work if fired from ahead of the enemy aircraft. This then, gave it an immensely greater hitting potential in air combat. The trouble was that it hadn't been tested in combat. The conventional Sidewinder had a low success rate – as poor as 18 per cent. Despite this 'all-aspect' advantage, and the claims of the missile's American manufacturer, Hercules, the combat effectiveness of this improved Sidewinder was still an unknown entity. The Falklands conflict would be its proving ground.

Sidewinder AIM-9L ('Lima') AAM	
Length	2.89m
Weight	86kg
Warhead	9.4kg
Guidance	Infrared or Laser-homing

The Sea Harrier also benefited from its revolutionary design. It was a vertical and/or short take-off and landing (or V/STOL) aircraft, which could operate from just about anywhere, regardless of the length of runway. The idea had first been pioneered in the early 1960s, and a prototype first made a carrier landing in 1963. By 1967 this had developed into the Hawker Siddeley Harrier, a small subsonic V/STOL ground-attack aircraft. In the early 1970s though, British Aerospace developed a version of it for use by the Royal Navy, which was reluctantly abandoning its fixed-wing carrier programme.

The Sea Harrier was first adopted by the Royal Navy in 1978, to serve aboard a new design of 'through deck cruiser'. These became the Invincible class of light carriers. When they entered service, these carriers were adapted by adding a curved 'ski jump' ramp at the forward end of the flight deck, to launch the V/STOL jet upwards, using its momentum to help it climb, thus saving on fuel and allowing a heavier payload to be carried. Effectively, the ski jump made the Sea Harrier much more effective.

The Sea Harrier was designed as joint fighter, reconnaissance and strike aircraft (FRS), so it was expected to fulfil a range of roles. Essentially the Sea Harrier was similar to the RAF's Harrier GR3 version, only it had a larger bubble canopy to increase visibility, and a slightly longer fuselage, to accommodate the Ferranti Blue Fox radar. When it was decided to reinforce the Task Force's air complement with several RAF GR3s, these were hurriedly adapted with the wherewithal to conduct carrier landings – a tailhook, fastening points to secure the aircraft, and a reinforced undercarriage. They were also modified to give them an aerial combat capability – modifications to allow the mounting of Sidewinders. In all, 14 Harrier GR3s would join the Task Force, and they would be used to conduct ground-attack missions, while the Sea Harriers provided air defence.

The Sea Harrier, like the Harrier GR3, was powered by a single Rolls-Royce Pegasus engine, which had four exit 'vector' nozzles, which could be angled, to reduce the flight

A Sea Harrier FRS.1, pictured in front of the island of HMS *Hermes*, identifiable by the pennant number 'R12'. This jet, part of the 800 Naval Air Squadron (NAS), is also identified as one of the carrier's embarked aircraft by the 'H' on the tail fin.

deck distance needed to take off. This, combined with the ski jump ramp, greatly boosted the aircraft's ability to carry a weapons payload. The vectored thrust nozzles also potentially gave these fighters a novel advantage. The thrust could be vectored in forward flight (VIFF), giving the pilots the ability to outmanoeuvre an enemy assailant. This thrust, would dramatically slow the Harrier, which wasn't what a pilot needed in a dogfight. The notion was untested in combat. As Flt Lt David Morgan of the RAF put it: 'Everybody had their own ideas on VIFF.' He felt that in all but very exceptional cases, it wouldn't be an advantage.

The Sea Harriers were embarked on two very different aircraft carriers. HMS *Hermes*, the larger of the two, had been laid down during World War II, but was only commissioned in 1959 as a Centaur-class light carrier, albeit one provided with an angled flight deck, to accommodate the jets of the era. For much of her life she operated Buccaneer strike aircraft and Sea Vixen fighters. Then, in the early 1970s, she was converted into a Commando carrier. This involved removing her steam catapults, which weren't needed, as she was now designed to operate nothing but helicopters. In 1976 *Hermes* was repurposed as an anti-submarine warfare carrier, equipped with ASW Sea King helicopters. However, the decommissioning of HMS *Ark Royal* in 1975 left the Royal Navy without any means to operate fixed-wing aircraft. So, in 1981, it was decided to fit her with a ski jump, to allow her to operate a handful of Sea Harriers.

This coincided with the commissioning of HMS *Invincible* in 1980, the first of three Invincible-class light carriers. She too was fitted with a ski ramp and was designed to carry an air wing of up to eight Sea Harriers and ten Sea King helicopters. While smaller than *Hermes*, *Invincible* was a powerful and well-designed carrier, protected by the latest Sea Dart anti-aircraft missile system, backed by fire control and long-range air-search radars. These two carriers then, would make up the Royal Navy's Carrier Battle Group, which was the heart of the hastily assembled Task Force. Incidentally, their Argentinian counterpart, the ARA *Veinticinco de Mayo*, was also British built, commissioned as the Colossus-class light carrier HMS *Venerable* in 1944. She then saw service in the Royal Netherlands Navy before being acquired by Argentina in 1968. She boasted steam catapults and an angled flight deck but was otherwise similar in size and design to *Hermes*. The big difference was that she carried A-4 Skyhawks, rather than the Sea Harrier.

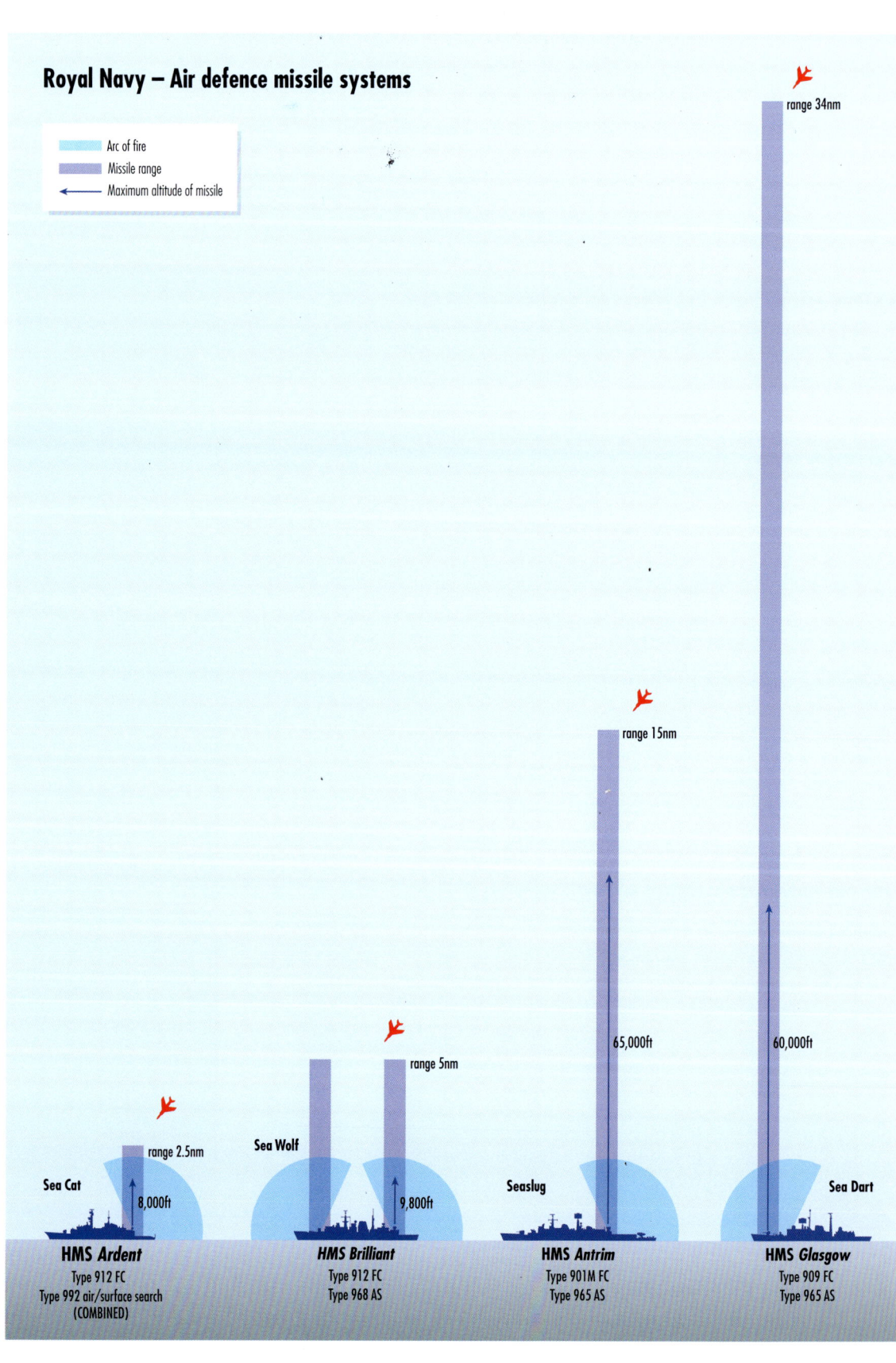

OPPOSITE MISSILE AIR DEFENCE OF ROYAL NAVY TASK FORCE: LAYOUT AND ARCS OF FIRE

Of the four air defence missile systems used in the Royal Navy's Task Force, two of them were obsolete, and of little practical value in a modern naval war. The close-range Sea Cat system was over two decades old, and while it had been modified and improved, it was still of very limited value, due to its short range, and the inability to track and launch multiple missiles. Equally antiquated was Seaslug, mounted in the fleet's ageing but elegant County-class destroyers, which were slow to bring into action, and lacked the accuracy provided by more modern systems.

Their replacements were Sea Wolf and Sea Dart. The first was another short-range system, albeit supported by modern fire control radar systems, and the ability to launch more than one missile at a time. Its longer-range version, Sea Dart, was a decade old by 1982, but it was effective, and its range made it a useful weapon in the right circumstances. Its weakness though, was its inability to effectively engage low-flying targets, such as low-flying fighter-bombers or sea-skimming missiles. During the war, Sea Dart was credited with shooting down six Argentinian jets and a helicopter, with HMS *Exeter* being the most successful Sea Dart armed warship in the Task Force. She though, carried a type 1022 radar, which was more accurate than the Type 965 fire control radars mounted in other Sea Dart armed vessels. Sea Wolf had three confirmed kills (all from HMS *Brilliant*), but the system also proved itself plagued by technical problems, which rendered it inoperable in key moments. While it was claimed that up to two hits were achieved using Sea Cat, these haven't been confirmed, and the downed Argentinian aircraft have also been claimed as 'kills' by others, including ground-launched SAM teams and warships firing short-range automatic weapons and small arms. Sea Cat was regarded as reliable though, and there is a high probability at least one of these shared hits was achieved by a Sea Cat fired from HMS *Argonaut*. Seaslug was fired by HMS *Antrim*, without scoring a hit, although her sister ship HMS *Glamorgan* used them in a shore bombardment capacity, during an attack on Port Stanley airfield.

These two Royal Navy carriers were priceless assets – the loss of either one of them would have an immense impact on the chance of success in the campaign. So, they were well protected by a screen of smaller warships; County-class and Type 42 destroyers; and Type 12, Type 21 and Type 22 frigates, supported by Royal Fleet Auxiliary (RFA) support vessels. The primary role of these warships, of course, was to protect the CVBG, using their anti-submarine and anti-aircraft weaponry, but they were also required to do the same for the Amphibious Landing Group, especially when Operation *Sutton* began – the planned amphibious landing on the Falkland Islands.

Their anti-aircraft weaponry varied considerably in effectiveness. It included the latest Sea Dart missile system carried in the Type 42s and *Invincible*, the shorter-range but highly effective Sea Wolf fitted on the Type 22s, and the old but still potentially useful Sea Slug system in the Counties. Then there was Sea Cat – an obsolete short-range anti-aircraft missile mounted in the other frigates, and in *Hermes*. It was due to be replaced by Sea Wolf, but this still hadn't happened before the ships were sent to the South Atlantic. So, forming an anti-

Sidewinder AIM-9L (Lima) air-to-air missile
Length 9ft 6in (2.89m)
Weight: 190lbs (86kg)
Warhead: 21lbs (9.4kg)
Guidance: Infrared or Laser-homing

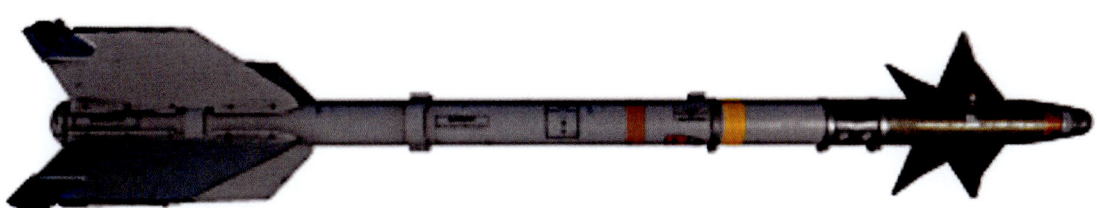

Sea Cat

A first-generation short-range SAM, first introduced in 1961, and produced in various versions since. Although obsolete by 1982, it was still mounted in many British warships:

Type 12 or Rothesay-class frigates: *Plymouth, Yarmouth*; Leander-class (Batch II) frigates: *Argonaut, Minerva, Penelope*; Type 21 or Amazon-class frigates: *Active, Alacrity, Ambuscade, Antelope, Ardent, Arrow, Avenger*; County-class destroyers: *Antrim, Glamorgan*, Fearless-class assault ships: *Fearless, Intrepid*; Centaur-class carriers: *Hermes*.

Propellant: Solid-fuel rocket. Weight: 150lb (68kg). Length: 4ft 10in (1.47m).

Guidance: Optical or radar-guided. Range: 2.5nm.
Missile speed: Mach 0.95. Warhead: High-explosive.

A four-missile launcher, usually mounted atop the vessel's hangar.

Versions used: GWS-20 (in Type 12s and Fearless class) used optical guidance only; GWS-22 (in Leanders, Counties and Hermes) relied on a Type 909 radar, with a detection range of 19nm. GWS-24 (in Type 21s) used a more efficient Type 912 radar, with a detection range of 21nm. However, only one missile was capable of being guided at a time.

Sea Wolf

The replacement for Sea Cat, produced by British Aerospace, and introduced in 1977. Essentially, it was a modern short-range air-defence system, and in 1982 it was primarily used to protect the carriers, with Type 22 frigates serving as protective 'gatekeepers'. It was a considerable improvement, but was only fitted in a relatively small number of warships in the Task Force:

Leander-class (Batch III) frigate: *Andromeda*; Type 22 frigates: *Brilliant, Broadsword*.

Propellant: Solid-fuel rocket. Weight: 180lb (82kg). Length: 6ft 3in (1.9m).

Guidance: Video monitor or radar-guided. Range: 5.4nm.
Missile speed: Mach 3.0. Warhead: High-explosive (contact or proximity detonation).

A six-missile launcher, mounted on foredeck (Type 22 class) or hangar roof (Leander class).

Version used: GWS-25, linked to Type 967 air-search radar and Type 968 short-range tracking radar, with fully automated guidance system based on the Type 912 fire-control radar, permitting control of two simultaneous missile launches (one on Leander class).

Seaslug

A first-generation long-range SAM, Sea Slug was first introduced in 1961, and designed to engage high-altitude aircraft. The Seaslug Mark II (GWS.2) was developed in 1965, and although completely obsolete, it was still in use in two ships of the Task Force. One of them even launched one in anger during the campaign, without achieving a hit.

County-class destroyers: *Antrim, Glamorgan*.

Propellant: Solid-fuel rocket with boosters.
Weight: 1,980lb (900kg). Length: 19ft 6in (5.9m).
Guidance: Beam-riding radar-guided. Range: 15nm.

Missile speed: Up to Mach 2.5.
Warhead: Continuous-rod explosive, with contact, proximity or operator-controlled detonation.

Mounted on a two-missile launcher, mounted on after deck of destroyer, served by an extensive network of magazine, component storage and missile handling space below decks. It utilized the elderly Type 901M fire-control radar, capable of beam-tracking, but by 1982 the County-class destroyers linked this to a more modern Type 965 air-search radar system.

Sea Dart

Sea Dart was a more versatile replacement for the obsolete Seaslug system, developed during the 1960s and first introduced in 1972. It was the navy's long-range SAM system, and was credited with seven confirmed 'kills' during the Falklands conflict.

Type 42 destroyers: *Cardiff, Coventry, Exeter, Glasgow, Sheffield*; Type 82 or Bristol-class destroyer: *Bristol*; Invincible-class aircraft carrier: *Invincible*.

Propellant: Ramjet with rocket booster.
Weight: 1,210lb (550kg). Length: 14ft 4in (4.4m).
Guidance: Semi-active radar-homing. Range: 34nm (63,000m) at high level; 11nm at low level.

Missile speed: Mach 3.0. Warhead: High-explosive (contact or proximity detonation).

A two-missile launcher, mounted on foredeck of all vessels.

Version used: Standard (Mod 0) version, linked to Type 965 air-search radar and Type 968 short-range tracking radar, with fully automated guidance system based on the Type 909 fire-control radar, permitting control of two simultaneous missile launches (one on Leander class). While the Type 965 was unable to accurately track low-flying targets, its replacement, the Type 1022 radar mounted in HMS *Exeter*, was much better and would eventually replace the earlier system.

aircraft screen around the Task Force was a complicated business, as the force commander, R Adm Sandy Woodward, had to consider the effectiveness of all these ships and systems when arranging his deployment. It did though, create a protective screen which, at least on paper, could prevent the loss or damage of these all-important carriers. It did though, by necessity, put the outer ring of escorts in harm's way.

No assessment of the Royal Navy's capability in the Falklands conflict can be considered without considering leadership and personnel. The Task Force was commanded by R Adm Sandy Woodward, a highly experienced naval officer who first joined the Royal Navy in 1946. He became a submariner and rose to command the nuclear submarine HMS *Warspite* before his promotion and a staff appointment. He subsequently commanded the destroyer HMS *Sheffield*, before becoming head of naval planning. He reached flag rank in 1981, and in April 1982 was given command of the CVBG, flying his flag in *Hermes*. Although *Invincible* was more modern, *Hermes* was better suited to accommodating his staff and carried a better communications suite. The CVBG was designated Task Group (TG) 317.8, which formed part of the larger Task Force (TF). In addition, Commodore Michael Clapp commanded the invasion task group, TG317.0, while the landing element of it became TG317.1.

The combined force, designated Task Force 317, was commanded by Admiral Sir John Fieldhouse. He joined the service in 1944, and he too specialized in submarines, receiving his first command in 1956. Further submarine commands followed, including the nuclear submarine HMS *Dreadnought*. After a spell as first lieutenant of *Hermes*, he was promoted to captain, and commanded a ballistic missile submarine flotilla. Various other commands followed before his promotion to flag rank in 1975, and vice admiral three years later. In 1981 Fieldhouse became a full admiral, and Commander-in-Chief Fleet (CINCFLEET). Then came the Falklands crisis, and his command of the Falklands Task Force. Both Fieldhouse and his deputy Woodward were intelligent men, with the experience and ability to plan and execute such a complex operation. If anyone could oversee the naval side of the recapture of the Falklands, it was these two men.

Unlike Woodward though, who was the man on the spot, Fieldhouse supervised the operation from his headquarters in Northwood, in North London. It was Fieldhouse then, who liaised with the Admiralty through the First Sea Lord, Admiral Sir Henry Leach, and with the War Cabinet, chaired by the Prime Minister Margaret Thatcher. Leach, who had seen action during the battle of North Cape in 1943, was adamant that the Falklands could and should be recaptured. It was he who convinced Thatcher that the sending of the Carrier Battle Group to the South Atlantic was the right course. Leach knew what his ships and men were capable of. The Royal Navy in 1982 was a service which had suffered at the hands of Thatcher's government, who had imposed draconian cuts upon it. However, he also realized that the Sea Harrier, combined with the new generation of anti-aircraft weaponry in the fleet's more modern ships, was effective enough to secure victory. Above all, he knew that the Royal Navy at that time was a highly professional force, with the expertise and morale needed to see the job done.

Vice Admiral Juan Jose Lombardo commanded the Argentinian naval opposition to the British Task Force. When at sea his flagship was the ARA *Veintecinco de Mayo*, and it was aboard her that he planned his counterstrike in early May – an operation postponed, and then cancelled following the sinking of the ARA *General Belgrano*.

CAMPAIGN OBJECTIVES
Struggle for the Falkland Islands

A Sea Harrier FRS.1 of 801 NAS is seen taking off from the 'ski jump' of HMS *Invincible* – a ramp which boosted the range and payload capacity of the aircraft. Also in the photograph are two RAF Harrier GR.3s of No. 1 (F) Sqn.

One of the weaknesses of the Argentinian invasion of the Falkland Islands was the speed with which the operation was conceived and executed. It was primarily a political initiative, imposed on the Argentinian armed forces by President Galtieri and his military junta. In December 1981, the unpopular military junta which had ruled Argentina since 1976 was replaced by a new one, led by General Leopoldo Galtieri. His junta also consisted of Brigadier Lami Dozo, who commanded the Argentine Air Force, and Admiral Jorge Anaya, Cdr-in-chief of the Argentine Navy. This new junta needed to establish itself, and show it planned to reform the economic and social stagnation which had marked the rule of its predecessors. So, encouraged primarily by Anaya, the junta decided to garner popular support in the country by seeking a military solution to the country's long-running territorial dispute with Britain over ownership of the Falkland Islands – an archipelago the Argentinians called the Malvinas.

The background

This then, was the climax of a protracted dispute over ownership of the islands between Britain and Argentina which had, effectively, rumbled on for a century and a half. It was the British who first discovered the archipelago and claimed ownership of it in 1690. However, it was the French who first established a settlement there in 1764 at Port Louis on East Falkland, 16 miles north-east of present-day Port Stanley. The following year the British arrived and established Port Egmont, on Saunders Island, off West Falkland. The French then sold their claim to the Spanish, who took over Port Louis, renaming it Port Soledad. In 1770, a Spanish expedition ejected the British from Port Egmont by force, and essentially the islands remained in Spanish hands. In 1816 though, when Argentina declared its independence from Spain, it also claimed possession of the 'Islas Malvinas'.

In 1829, the British re-asserted their older claim of sovereignty, and in 1833 the islands were formally reclaimed by Britain. By 1845, when Port Stanley was established, the Falklands were firmly established as a British colony, despite occasional protests from the Argentinians.

A Sea Harrier on the flight deck of HMS *Hermes* being waved off. An added advantage of the 'ski jump' at the flight deck's forward end was that it allowed the rapid launch of multiple aircraft, without the long delays involved if steam-powered catapults had been required.

This continued until the 1960s, when Argentina persuaded the United Nations to regard sovereignty of the archipelago as an international issue. By then, the British claim was firmly underpinned by their long-established governorship of the islands, stretching back more than a century. The will of the Falkland islanders themselves was also considered important, as they were adamant that they wished to remain British. Diplomatic talks continued, with the Argentinian position hardening occasionally, as the concern proved a useful political issue, capable of rallying Argentinian popular support. Finally, in early 1982, the Galtieri junta decided to reclaim the islands by force.

This invasion, codenamed *Operación Rosario*, was preceded by a couple of less dramatic moves, to test British resolve. As far back as 1976, the previous military junta in Argentina had ordered a scientific station to be established on Thule Island, in the South Sandwich Islands. Located midway between the Falklands and Antarctica, this remote and bleak cluster of three tiny volcanic islands was officially considered British territory, as a dependency of the Falklands. The British government complained but did nothing else about it. This inaction prompted an even more audacious land grab on 19 March 1982, when a small Argentinian civilian force established itself at Thule on South Georgia, a small island 870 miles east of the Falklands, and the home of a British Antarctic Survey (BAS) team. Its base at Grytviken had previously been a whaling station. Diplomatic negotiations followed, but the Argentinians refused to leave.

At the request of the survey team, the ice patrol ship HMS *Endurance* put into Grytviken, on 24 March – a week before *Operación Rosario* began. Capt Nick Barker of *Endurance* had his embarked Royal Marine detachment establish an observation post overlooking Thule, 17 miles from Grytviken. The following day, an Argentinian icebreaker, the ARA *Bahia Paraiso*, arrived off Leith, marines were landed, and her helicopter began shadowing *Endurance*. A diplomatic solution to this international incident was still being pursued a week later, when the invasion of the Falklands got underway.

Argentinian intentions

Operación Rosario was a well-planned and reasonably well-executed invasion. On 26 March, as two Argentinian frigates were on their way to deal with the situation on South Georgia, a large part of the Argentinian fleet put to sea, including the carrier *Veinticinco de Mayo*. This was ostensibly a naval exercise, but in fact it was the build-up to *Rosario*. At this point, although Admiral Anaya's operation had been put into motion, President Galtieri had still not committed to the invasion. He finally did though, that evening, and it was scheduled to begin on 29 March. By then though, a front of bad weather was passing through the region, and so the operation was postponed by two days. It was then scheduled to commence on Friday 2 April. The invasion ran relatively smoothly, with advance parties landed on East Falkland, to carry out a pre-emptive attack on Moody Brook barracks, to the west of Port Stanley. At 06.00 Argentinian marines landed at York Bay, near Stanley airfield, and they advanced on the town, harried by the 70-strong detachment of Royal Marines stationed there. The British force was hopelessly outnumbered though and fell back on Government House. They lay down their arms at 09.30, and Stanley fell to the Argentinians.

The Argentinians then reinforced their troops in the Falklands, and on 7 April Maj Gen Mario Menéndez was appointed as the island's military governor. Martial law was imposed, and a number of Falklanders were confined or deported as the Argentinians asserted their authority over the civil population. Meanwhile, on South Georgia Argentinian marines were landed to capture Grytviken, which was eventually captured despite a spirited defence by the small Royal Marine detachment there. During the Grytviken engagement, the corvette ARA *Guerrico* was badly damaged, and an Argentinian helicopter was shot down. These were merely opening shots in a conflict that would last for ten more weeks.

The Argentinians never expected the British to send a Task Force to recover the Falkland Islands. So, President Galtieri's military junta had no plan in place to defend the Falkland Islands – or the 'Islas Malvinas', as the Argentinians now called them. There was no economic justification for this British response, and it was considered highly unlikely the British would fight for such a strategically unimportant possession, located 8,000 miles away. The junta failed to appreciate the British desire to defend their sovereign territory, and to punish the aggressors. Instead, the junta had been preparing for diplomatic talks, which they expected would lead to a formal transfer of the archipelago's sovereignty. In effect, the Argentinians completely underestimated the British will to go to war over the Falklands. As a result, no

An Israeli-built IAI-1 Dagger, the Israeli version of the French Mirage 5 multi-fighter, deployed in Argentina's Grupo 6 de Caza, based at Río Gallegos airbase. This aircraft (C-418) was marked with four ship 'kills', purely for publicity purposes, to represent the victories claimed by the entire group during the conflict.

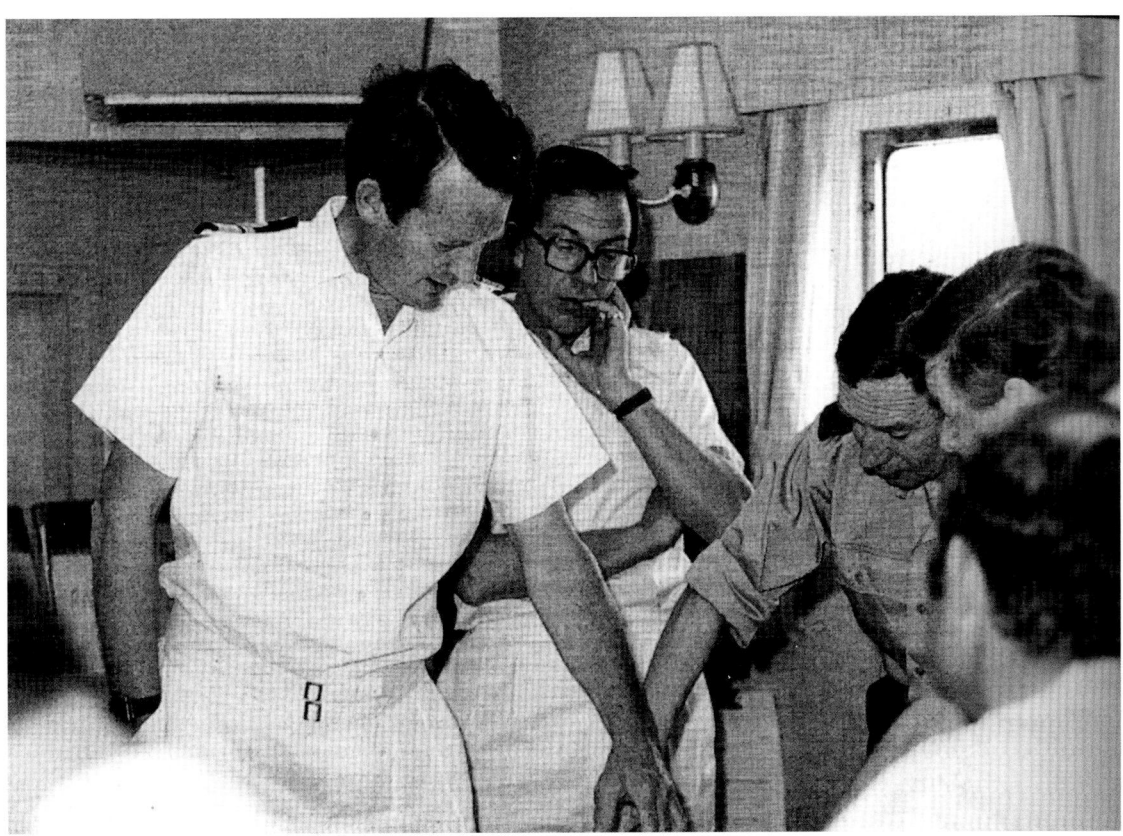

In early April, during the voyage to Ascension Island, R Adm Sandy Woodward held a series of planning meetings with his senior captains and staff. Here, Woodward (centre), pointing at the chart, is seen holding one in the Flag Operations Room aboard HMS *Glamorgan*. To his right his Staff Officer Operations, Cdr Jeremy Sanders, an expert in naval tactics.

military appreciation had been drawn up for the defence of the Falkland Islands before the Task Force sailed. Similarly, there was no strategic plan in place to counter any British naval deployment into the South Atlantic.

After it became clear that the British were actually coming, the Argentinian military should have worked closely with Maj Gen Menéndez to develop a well-prepared and detailed plan for the effective defence of the Falklands. To recapture the Falklands, the British needed to undertake an amphibious landing. A successful Argentinian defence would have been possible if Menéndez and his superiors had carried out a thorough evaluation of the islands, to determine possible landing sites, and to prepare defences of these sites. It appears that this was never undertaken. Instead, the Argentinians reinforced their garrison, which, for the most part, was concentrated on East Falkland, with the bulk of the defenders concentrated around Stanley. Instead, it was felt that the Argentine Navy and Air Force were powerful enough to defeat the British Task Force while it was still at sea, or at least before it could carry out any amphibious landing. Essentially, it was left to the Argentine Air Force and the air wing of the Argentine Navy to defend the Falklands.

This lack of strategic preparation would cost the Argentinians dearly. While much of this was due to a misreading of the political signals emanating from London, and an underestimation of Britain's resolve to recover the islands, there was still no real excuse for the lack of an operational plan for the defence of the Falkland Islands, or a strategic plan to counter any British naval deployment in the region. The best that was done, apart from the establishment of defensive positions on East Falkland, and the reinforcement of Menéndez's Falklands Military Garrison, was the preparation for naval air strikes by Brigadier Crespo's Southern Air Force, and his liaison with Vice Admiral Lombardo's South Atlantic Military Theatre to ensure the air force and the navy worked together to prevent any amphibious

Air-to-air missile systems

*Accuracy is greatly increased if AAM launched from rear 180° of target.

Zone of vulnerability

Zone of vulnerability*

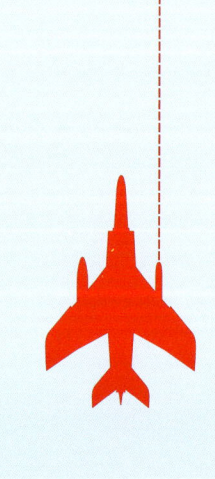

Firing a 'rear aspect' AAM

Firing on 'all-round aspect' AAM

Of all the dogfights fought during the conflict, the only hits scored by air-to-air missiles (AAMs) were from Sidewinder AIM-9Ls launched by Sea Harriers. These accounted for a total of 17 'kills' and two shared 'kills' – a success rate of 80 per cent. The Sea Harrier might have been the most successful jet fighter of the conflict, but it owed much of its success to its improved 'all aspect' Sidewinder.

OPPOSITE AIR-TO-AIR MISSILE SYSTEMS

invasion. It was clear though, at least to Lombardo, that their real objective was the British aircraft carriers. By sinking them, then the safety of the Falkland Islands would be assured. This then, at least until the British amphibious landing got underway, was the primary aim of the Argentine military.

British plans

Ironically, this lack of an overall plan was mirrored on the British side. When the Task Force sailed on 5 April, despite a Carrier Battle Group being sent, and an amphibious group assembled, there was still no plan in place to recover the Falklands. That would be developed during the voyage south. For R Adm Woodward, everything hinged on the air campaign. This, in turn, meant his two carriers and their embarked Sea Harriers. Given the disparity in numbers of aircraft, with an estimated 120 Argentinian front-line jets facing 20 British ones, the outlook was not ideal. Still, the Royal Navy and RAF pilots in the two carriers had faith in their aircraft, while their squadron commanders felt that they would be able to provide air protection for the Task Force. This was crucial as Woodward understood the loss of one or both carriers would make the successful recovery of the Falklands all but impossible.

So, the first British priority was to ensure the protection of the Carrier Battle Group. Its survival was considered a vital prerequisite for the deployment of the amphibious group. Without air cover, it was felt that there was little chance that the landing would be successful. This, then, created a second aim – the protection of the landing force during the amphibious landing on the Falklands. Once the military force was safely established ashore, then the focus would shift. From that point on, it would become the focus of military attention. This meant the supply of the British force ashore, the provision of air cover for it, as well as its support by the Task Force in the provision of naval gunfire and air strikes, to help the military accomplish their mission. The mission, of course, would be

HMS *Hermes*, pictured from the end of her 'ski jump, as she steamed south towards the Falklands. This was a crucial time for the CVBG, as both the flight deck personnel, and the Sea Harrier and Sea King air crews had to fully prepare themselves and their aircraft for the coming conflict. Her commanding officer, Capt Lin Middleton was a former naval aviator, and so was well attuned to the needs of his embarked air wing.

ORDER OF BATTLE

Argentinian forces

AIR FORCE ASSETS (*FUERZA AÉREA ARGENTINA*)
In April 1982 the FAA had an operational total of 45 Skyhawk A-4 attack aircraft (both B and C versions), 37 Dagger and 17 Mirage III fighter-bombers, ten Canberra light bombers and approximately 35 Pucará light ground support aircraft, which could at a pinch be used in an anti-shipping role. These were supported by seven C-130 Hercules transport planes, two C-130 Hercules air-refuelling tankers, and an assortment of civil aircraft, repurposed as military transports. In addition, the FAA maintained a number of helicopters. These were distributed around the airfields, as shown below. The number of aircraft listed is considered accurate for 1 May 1983, although the exact number of operational aircraft varied slightly, due to availability, mechanical reliability and losses. Also included here are land-based naval air assets.
BAM = *Base Aérea Militar* (Military Air Base)
BAN = *Base Aéronaval* (Naval Air Base)

Almirante Zar BAN, Trelew, Chubut Province
8 Canberras (Grupo 2 de Bombardeo) later relocated to Río Gallegos

Comodoro Rivadavia BAM, Chubut Province
7 Mirage IIIA (I Escuadrón, Grupo 8 de Caza)
1 FMA IA Pucará (Grupo 4 de Ataque)
2 Learjets (Grupo 1 de Aérofotografico (*Escuadrón Fenix*), an air photograph unit)
Note: This was also the base of the Southern Air Force.

Airfield San Julián, Puerto San Julián, Santa Cruz Province
14 1A1 Dagger (Escuadrón II (*Martinette*), Grupo 6 de Caza)
16 A-4C Skyhawk (Grupo 4 de Caza)

Río Gallegos BAM, Río Gallegos, Santa Cruz Province
8 Mirage IIIA (II Escuadrón, Grupo 8 de Caza)
30 A-4B Skyhawks (Grupo 5 de Caza)
FMA IA Pucará (Grupo 4 de Ataque)
There was an air traffic control centre there, and it was also the base of the Naval Exploration Squadron, consisting of two Grumman S-2 Tracker ASW aircraft (*Escuadrilla Antisubmarina*). The C-130H tankers were also based there.

HMS *Invincible*, the first of a class of three light carriers, was the only one in commission when the Falklands conflict began. She had been designed as an anti-submarine warfare (ASW) helicopter carrier, but while under construction she was modified to handle Sea Harriers.

Almirante Quijada NAS, Río Grande, Tierre del Fuego Province
13 1A1 Daggers (Escuadrón III (*Las Avutardas Salvajes*), Grupo 6 de Caza)
8 A-4Q Skyhawks (once landed from the ARA *Veinticinco de Mayo*)
4 Super Étendards (2 Escuadrilla de Caza y Ataque)
Also based there were two SP-2H Neptune long-range marine patrol aircraft (*Escuadrilla de Exploración, ARA*).

In the Falkland Islands, as part of the *Guarnición Militar Malvinas*, the following were stationed at Port Stanley, and at the secondary small airfields at Goose Green and Pebble Island:
24 FMA IA Pucarás (Grupo 3 de Ataque)
6 Aermacchi MB-339As (1 Escuadrilla de Ataque, ARA)
4 T-34 Mentors (4 Escuadrilla de Ataque, ARA)

NAVAL ASSETS (*ARMADA REPÚBLICA ARGENTINA*)
Task Force 20 (Vice Admiral Juan Lombardo) Covering Force
Aircraft carrier: *Veinticinco de Mayo* [The '25 May'] (flagship)
Destroyers: *Comodoro Py, Hipólito Bouchard, Piedra Buena, Segui*
Tanker: *Punta Medanos*
Veinticinco de Mayo – Air Wing:
8 A-4Q Skyhawks (3 Escuadrilla de Caza y Ataque)
Supported by six S-2E Tracker ASW aircraft (*Escuadrilla Antisubmarina*) and five Sikorsky SH-3 Sea King ASW helicopters (*2 Escuadrilla de Helicopteros*).
Note: Later in the conflict these aircraft were disembarked and sent to land-based airfields.
Task Force 40 (Rear Admiral Jorge Gualter Allara) Amphibious Support Group
Destroyers: *Santísima Trinidad* (flagship), *Hercules*
Frigates: *Drummond, Granville*
Submarine: *Santa Fe*
Task Force 40.1 (Rear Admiral of Marines Carlos Busser) Amphibious Group
Landing ship: *Cabo San Antonio* (flagship)
Icebreaker: *Almirante Irizar*
Transport ship: *Isla de los Estados*
Task Force 60 South Georgia Invasion Force
Frigate: *Guerrico*
Icebreaker: *Bahia Paraiso*

British forces

NAVAL ASSETS (ROYAL NAVY)
Task Group 317.8 Carrier Battle Group (CVBG)
Aircraft carriers:
Hermes (Centaur-class aircraft carrier)
Invincible (Invincible-class light aircraft carrier)
Hermes – Air Wing:
12 Sea Harriers (800 NAS)
9 HAS.5 Sea King ASW helicopters (826 NAS)
Invincible – Air Wing:
8 Sea Harriers (801 NAS)
11 HAS.5 Sea King ASW Helicopters (820 NAS)
Destroyers: *Antrim, Glamorgan* (County class)
  Bristol (Type 82 or Bristol class)
  Cardiff, Coventry, Exeter, Glasgow, Sheffield (Type 42 class)
Frigates: *Brilliant, Broadsword* (Type 22 class)
  Active, Alacrity, Ambuscade, Antelope, Ardent, Arrow, Avenger (Type 21 or Amazon class)
  Andromeda, Argonaut, Minerva, Penelope (Leander class)
  Plymouth, Yarmouth (Type 12 or Rothesay class)

In addition, other Sea King, Wessex, Lynx and Wasp helicopters were embarked in the warships of the Task Force:
  Wessex 3 ASW helicopters in County-class destroyers
  Wessex 5 transport helicopters in Fearless-class landing ships
  Lynx or Wasp helicopters in other destroyers or frigates (Wasps only in Type 12 frigates)

Capt Jeremy Black, commander of HMS *Invincible*, assisted R Adm Woodward by supervising the air defence of the CVBG during the campaign. This involved both the deployment of the Combat Air Patrols, as well as the air defences of the warships surrounding the carriers themselves. It was a key job, which Black conducted with great skill.

the defeat of the Argentinian garrison on the Falklands and the recapture of Port Stanley. In other words, the centre of gravity – in modern military terms – would shift twice during the campaign. However, the protection of the Carrier Battle Group would remain a vital part of the whole operation.

For this though, Woodward was sanguine that his carriers would be as well protected as was possible, given the naval resources available to him. In all, eight destroyers and 15 frigates would form part of the Task Force. While these had a wide range of capabilities, and included older as well as modern vessels, taken together, and deployed to their best advantage, they could create a protective ring around the carriers that would be extremely hard to breach. In addition, properly guided by modern long-range air-search radar, the Sea Harriers could provide effective air protection over the carriers, while the embarked helicopters in the Task Force would also play their part in ensuring protection against Argentinian submarines. In addition, half of the Royal Navy's fleet of nuclear attack submarines would be on hand to counter any sortie by the Argentinian surface fleet. So, with the carriers protected, Woodward's Sea Harriers could begin to gain air superiority over the region, which in turn would allow the amphibious element of the Task Group to carry out its own mission. Much though, depended on the effectiveness of the Sea Harrier.

As the Task Force sailed south, and plans were developed in more detail, two developments would exert a major influence on what lay ahead. First, the British began building up Ascension Island as a forward base, and a stepping stone between Britain and the Falklands. This small British-governed island lay 3,700nm from Britain, on the northern edge of the South Atlantic. Throughout April the RAF reinforced Wideawake airfield there, whose 10,000ft-long runway permitted the use of large aircraft, including Hercules transport planes, which allowed the build-up of supplies, equipment and personnel before the Task Force reached the island. Ascension could be used as a base for long-range Nimrod reconnaissance aircraft, which could range as far as the Falklands, and the RAF's ageing Vulcan bombers, which could also reach the archipelago. This meant that the RAF could play its part in the campaign to recover the Falklands.

On 12 April the British government declared the establishment of a Maritime Exclusion Zone (MEZ) around the Falklands, forming a circle around the islands with a radius of 200 miles. This was supported by a declaration that any Argentinian warship or auxiliary that entered the MEZ was liable to be attacked by a British nuclear submarine. In effect, they were drawing a line around the Falklands, emphasizing Britain's right to defend the area. This was a declaration which was fully recognized in international maritime law. On 23 April, as the Task Force drew closer to the war zone, the Argentinian government was informed that any Argentinian ship or aircraft that posed a threat to British forces could be attacked.

Then, on 30 April, as the Task Force reached a point 250 miles north of the Falklands, the British declared a Total Exclusion Zone (TEZ). This was a modification of the MEZ, but this time the warning was more comprehensive. Now, any sea vessel or aircraft that entered the TEZ would be liable to be attacked without warning, regardless of its nationality. It would be put into practice two days later, when the cruiser ARA *General Belgrano* was torpedoed and sunk by the nuclear-powered attack submarine HMS *Conqueror*. Despite a furore afterwards, this action was deemed perfectly legitimate under international law. The Argentine Navy fully understood the risk. This sinking though, marked the real start of the naval war, and the air campaign that followed. Finally, on 7 May, the TEZ was extended to the edge of Argentinian coastal waters, 12 miles off the Argentinian coast. This, more than anything, was designed to increase the threat posed by the Royal Navy's 'hunter killer' submarines. However, the whole process of delineating exclusion zones served another purpose. It marked the area of the South Atlantic that was considered a war zone by both sides. It meant that from 30 April on, the gloves were off.

THE CAMPAIGN
The air war over the South Atlantic

As the CVBG approached the Falklands, the two Sea Harrier squadrons conducted daily air combat and interception exercises, to help bring the squadrons and the carrier crews up to a full war footing. The 8012 NAS pictured here, taking off from HMS *Invincible* was lost on 6 May, in what was probably a mid-air collision.

The story did the rounds that for years the Royal Navy had planned to fight a war against the Soviet Union, with the main theatre being off Norway. Instead, it was called up to head off to the South Atlantic. When asked what initial planning was involved to dispatch the Task Force to the Falklands, Admiral Fieldhouse quipped that it was simple. They simply used the Norwegian plan; only, instead of turning left after leaving Portsmouth, they turned right. This, of course, while containing a small kernel of truth, didn't take into account the immense effort it took to assemble the Task Force and send it on its way. For five days, Portsmouth Naval Dockyard was one of the busiest places in the country, with stores, weapons, crew and specialist engineers and technicians working long hours to prepare the ships for sea. Inevitably, some things were forgotten, or there were last-minute vital additions. Three more helicopters were embarked on *Fearless*. When the two carriers slipped out of Portsmouth Harbour, they were cheered off by crowds of well-wishers. One pilot aboard *Hermes* quipped, 'I suppose the Spanish Armada enjoyed a send-off like this!'

The voyage south

Elements of the Task Force departed from several ports. For instance, the frigates *Alacrity* and *Antelope* sailed from Devonport, accompanied by the RFA tanker *Olmeda*, to join the carriers at sea. In addition, 3 Commando Bde was sailing in its own hastily assembled group, which was centred around the assault ship *Fearless*, and included four landing ships, two chartered transport ships (including the liner *Canberra*), and the RFA store ship *Stromness*.

By 6 April, as the CVBG headed through the English Channel, various other strands were being pulled together by the Ministry of Defence. These included the frigates *Broadsword* and *Yarmouth* to join the Task Force from Gibraltar, and the nuclear submarines *Conqueror*, *Spartan* and *Splendid* to head south too. A NATO exercise, Operation *Spring Train*, had been taking part in the Eastern Atlantic, and several warships were pulled out of it and sent to join the Task Force instead. These included the County-class destroyers *Antrim* and *Glamorgan*,

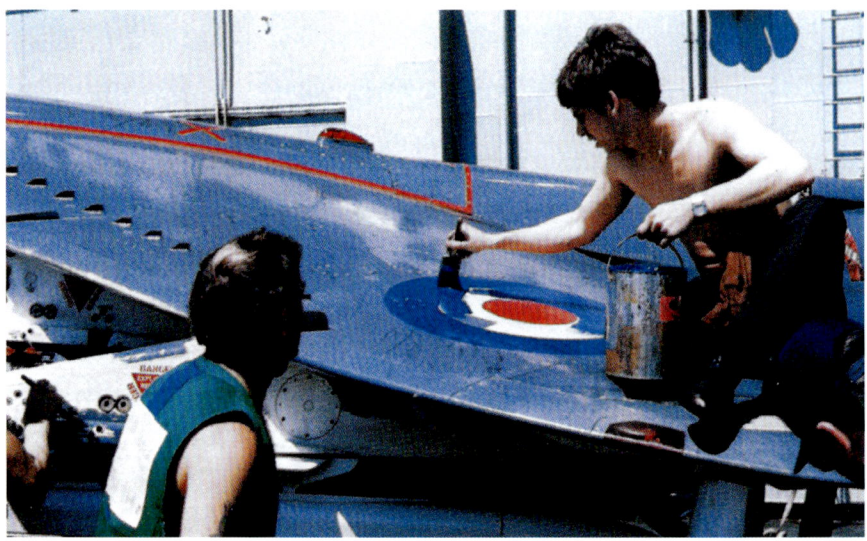

During the voyage south from Ascension Island to the Falklands, the embarked Sea Harriers of 800 and 801 NAS were repainted, toning down their markings and roundels to make the SHARs less conspicuous. Here, a three-colour roundel on an 800 NAS is turned into a two-colour one, using a 3in paintbrush.

the Type 42 destroyers *Coventry*, *Glasgow* and *Sheffield*, the Type 22 frigate *Brilliant* and the ageing Rothesay-class frigate *Plymouth*. Other scattered warships and RFAs also received their sailing orders.

By Good Friday, 9 April, the Task Force was beginning to coalesce. *Antrim* and *Plymouth* and the RFA *Tidespring* were formed into a South Georgia Task Group, with a Royal Marine Commando company embarked. Meanwhile, although other support vessels were still leaving Britain, and other warships were preparing to reinforce the British armada, attention now turned to Ascension Island, some 800 miles off the West African coast and 1,200 miles from Brazil. From 5 April the first Nimrod maritime patrol aircraft arrived at RAF Wideawake airbase there, allowing patrols to range far into the South Atlantic. Six Victor replenishment tankers also arrived, to help extend these patrols as far as the Falklands and South Georgia.

It took 11 days for the carriers to reach Ascension. The time was spent conducting exercises and drills and preparing the ships and aircraft for war. For the air crews, this also meant practising and perfecting manoeuvres and tactics, and getting used to the live firing of their weapons, including Sidewinders. Airborne radars were fine-tuned, while in warship operations rooms, teams practised the direction of air missions. Finally, the Sea Harriers were repainted, greying out their white undersides, and toning down the nationality roundels. During the voyage south, *Invincible* even ran out of grey paint.

Ascension was reached on 16 April, by which time an advanced group of three destroyers and four frigates was already heading through the South Atlantic. Even farther ahead was the South Georgia Task Group, led by the *Antrim*, which rendezvoused with the ice patrol vessel *Endurance*. Even closer, though, were three British nuclear attack submarines – *Splendid*, *Spartan* and *Conqueror*. When the Maritime Exclusion Zone was created on 12 April, they were approaching the Falklands, ready to enforce the exclusion if ordered.

On reaching South Georgia on 21 April, Special Air Service (SAS) groups were landed to observe the Argentinian garrison, despite a raging ice storm. The arrival of the Argentinian diesel submarine *Santa Fe* on 23 April posed a problem, but two days later she was detected by *Antrim* and depth-charged and damaged by Antrim's helicopter. The submarine limped into Grytviken, where she was damaged in attacks by British helicopters. Her crew abandoned the boat. Then, under cover of a naval bombardment, British forces landed near Grytviken, and the Argentinian garrison surrendered without firing a shot. The following day the Argentinian garrison at Leith also surrendered. South Georgia was now back in British hands. The only casualty in the whole operation was a sailor from the *Santa Fe*.

The Royal Navy's Type 21 frigate entered service from the mid-1970s, having been built in private shipyards, to reduce their cost. They were general-purpose escorts, armed with a mixed bag of weapons. For their air defence, they relied on the antiquated Sea Cat system, with a launcher mounted atop the hangar, a 4.5in /Mark 8 gun, and 20mm Oerlikons. This vessel is HMS *Arrow*, commanded by Cdr Paul Bootherstone.

From 19 April on, as the Amphibious Task Group assembled off Ascension, it took on stores and men before heading south to the Falklands. On 21 April, a Sea Harrier from 800 NAS intercepted an Argentinian Boeing maritime patrol aircraft. At the time, no hostile action was allowed, so the aircraft escaped. It had though, spotted the British force. Other sightings would follow, until on 26 April the British changed the rules of engagement. Now, enemy aircraft would be intercepted and shot down. By then the CVBG was east of Buenos Aires and approaching the MEZ from the north-east. The two carriers were now accompanied by four destroyers (*Coventry*, *Glamorgan*, *Glasgow* and *Sheffield*), four frigates (*Alacrity*, *Arrow*, *Broadsword* and *Yarmouth*) and the RFA ships *Olmeda* and *Resource*.

The Argentinians knew the British Task Force was approaching. So, in preparation, COAN's Super Étendards were moved to Río Grande, while the Argentinian carrier was prepared for active operations. On 29 April, Task Force 79 put to sea, built around the *Veinticinco de Mayo*. The force was split into three parts: the carrier, its escorts and a covering force (designated TF 79.4). This meant that as the British CVBG entered the TEZ, the Argentine Navy would be around 400 miles to the north-west of it, while a southern group led by the cruiser ARA *General Belgrano* left Ushuaia in Tierra del Fuego, and moved into position to the south of the archipelago. The object was to catch the British between two naval pincers.

Meanwhile, *Brilliant* and *Plymouth* headed north-west to join them from South Georgia, while *Antrim* and the RFA *Tidespring* remained off South Georgia, preparing to escort Argentinian POWs back to Ascension. On 30 April, when the MEZ was replaced by a TEZ, Woodward's CVBG was just off its eastern side. He planned to enter the MEZ the following day. That placed his carriers within striking range of the Falkland Islands. The British were about to strike back.

Saturday 1 May

Air operations from the British carriers were timed to coincide with *Black Buck 1*, an air strike on Port Stanley airfield carried out by a Vulcan strategic bomber. It left Ascension the previous evening and was refuelled during the flight. It arrived over the airfield at 04.45 and dropped 21 1,000lb anti-runway bombs over the target from 10,000ft. By the time the Argentinian AA guns opened up, the Vulcan was already on her long flight home. The *Black Buck* operation was a monumental effort, involving a complex chain of mid-air refuelling

An FMA IA-58 Pucará (A-555), of the Grupo 3 de Ataque, pictured in this snapshot by an Argentinian airman on BAM *Condor* (Goose Green airfield). On 28 May this aircraft was shot down by fire from 2 Para Regt, but the pilot, Lt Cruzado, managed to eject. After that, the remaining serviceable aircraft at Goose Green were evacuated to Port Stanley.

operations. As Ascension and Port Stanley were 3,886 miles apart, this was the longest bombing mission ever carried out.

Black Buck though, was less effective than the RAF had hoped. Only one of the bombs hit the runway. This though, left a large crater, which would take time to repair. In the meantime, the runway couldn't be used by anything other than the smallest Argentinian jets. The mission was a morale-booster for the Falkland islanders, as it showed they hadn't been abandoned. It also demonstrated Britain's ability to reach the Falklands, and even Argentina itself. For R Adm Woodward, *Black Buck* was a double-edged sword. News of the attack was a welcome tonic. However, it also meant that when it was his pilots' turn to attack the same target, the enemy would be fully alert.

The CVBG was 100 miles east-north-east of Port Stanley. Woodward planned to launch a series of attacks on both Port Stanley and Goose Green airfields. Of the two, the Port Stanley attack was the largest, involving nine of 800 NAS's Sea Harriers, divided into two strikes. The first of four aircraft was to make a low-level bombing attack on the airfield from the north-east. Then, when the Argentinians were distracted, the remaining five would attack from the north-west. The remaining three Sea Harriers from 800 NAS would attack Goose Green, in a low-level attack from the north. While this was taking place, 801 NAS embarked in *Invincible* would send up six Sea Harriers, to fly a combat air patrol (CAP) to the east of the Falklands.

The first of the strike aircraft took off from *Hermes* at 07.48, some 15 minutes before dawn. After forming up, the two Port Stanley strikes made landfall off East Falkland at 08.05, 20 miles north of their objective, and split into smaller groups. The first to reach the target was Red Section, led by Lt Cdr Tony Ogilvy. Each of his four Sea Harriers carried three 1,000lb radar-fused bombs, set to detonate over the target. This was a 'toss-bomb' strike. The jets flew in low, and then, on reaching a point three miles from the airfield, the Sea Harriers pulled into a climb, then released their bombs.

They then turned away to the south-east. Their target was the AA defences around the western side of the airfield. These AA guns opened up just as the jets turned away, and Tigercat SAMs were launched at the jets. The detonation of the bombs added to the confusion, which in turn allowed Black Section to make its approach undetected.

Led by Lt Cdr Andy Auld, the five Harriers of Black Section came in low from the west. This was a 'lay down' strike, using cluster bombs to hit the airfield's maintenance and storage areas, and any aircraft on the ground. Lt Cdr Mike Blissett, who led the strike, recalled: 'There was a lot of fire from just off the western end of the runway, and more from the hills to the south-west, all coming towards me.' The jets jinked to either side to throw off the Argentinian gunners, then made their bombing run. Blissett released his bombs over the airfield buildings, then sped away. Three other Harriers dropped cluster bombs, while Flt Lt Bertie Penfold bombed the runway. Two of Penfold's bombs hit the runway, adding to the damage caused by the Vulcan earlier that morning. The cluster bombs fragmented all around the airfield, causing damage to airfield facilities, and a few aircraft.

Flt Lt Dave Morgan was the last pilot to carry out his attack. He saw bombs exploding and AA fire all over the place. His Sea Harrier was hit just as he was about to release his bombs, but he kept going and dropped his payload. He banked away, dropping chaff (radar-reflective foil strips) to foil a ground radar which had locked on to him. Then he followed the others as they raced back towards *Hermes*. Surprisingly, despite the heavy AA fire thrown up, his was the only strike aircraft that was damaged that morning.

Meanwhile, the three remaining Sea Harriers of Tartan section were approaching Goose Green from the north-west. The strike, led by Lt Cdr 'Fred' Frederiksen, came in fast and low, taking the defenders by surprise, and ground fire was minimal. On the runway a Pucará preparing to take off was destroyed, and its pilot was killed. Two other Pucarás were also damaged. Overall, it was a successful morning for 800 NAS. It also sent a message to the Argentinian garrison that the British had arrived.

More importantly, this marked a start of the real air campaign. So, even as the ground-attack strikes were underway, other Sea Harriers were sent aloft, to fly CAP missions to the west of the Task Force. At the same time, Sea King helicopters from *Hermes* conducted ASW sweeps around the Task Force, after a report that the Argentinian submarine *San Luis* was in the area. Everyone fully expected an Argentinian response to the raids. Sure enough, it came. Even before the Sea Harriers struck, two Argentinian Daggers were sent out to locate the British. When they failed to sight anything though, they returned to base.

Afterwards, a series of poorly coordinated sorties was made, drawing on Canberras of Grupo 2, Skyhawks of Grupo 4 and 5, Daggers of Grupo 6 and Mirages of Grupo 8. The first of these came in the late morning, when six Mirage fighters were detected on British radar, approaching from the west. At the time the CAP screen consisted of just two Sea Harriers, flown by Lt Cdr John Eyton-Jones and Flt Lt Paul Barton. They intercepted the attackers

The British-built Argentinian aircraft carrier ARA *Veintecinco de Mayo* was to have carried out an air strike on the British Task Force using her embarked A-4Q Skyhawks, but bad weather led to the strike's postponement. Then, following the sinking of the ARA *General Belgrano*, the carrier was withdrawn from operations, and her aircraft redeployed to land-based airfields.

A 1,000lb bomb, inscribed with the name of its intended target, awaiting the arming of the A-4Q Skyhawks of the 3 Escuadrilla de Caza y Ataque on board the ARA *Veintecinco de Mayo*, before the aborted air strike against the British Task Force planned for 2 May.

but found they were flying too high to engage. However, the Mirages didn't press on after being intercepted, but turned around and headed home. The first real clash, though, came from the Argentinian aircraft based at Port Stanley.

At noon a naval bombardment force approached Port Stanley from the east, to shell the airfield. Three T-34 Mentors of 4 Escuadrilla skirted the craters in the runway and took off, to launch a strike on the three British ships. They were intercepted by two Sea Harriers flown by Cdr 'Sharkey' Ward and Lt Mike Watson of 801 NAS. Wisely, the little Argentinian prop-planes dodged into the clouds and withdrew. A lull followed, which lasted until 15.40, when the Mirages of Grupo 3 found themselves in contact with the British CAP screen.

To the west of the Task Force, Flt Lt Barton and Lt Steve Thomas were directed towards the wave of Mirages approaching from the west, and spotted them at a range of 8 miles, at 12,000ft. Thomas headed straight towards them, while Barton worked his way round to the right – the north – to come in behind them. The British pilots thought the echelon formation

Argentinian naval pilots of the 3 Escuadrilla de Caza y Ataque, pictured in front of their A-4Q Skyhawk strike aircraft at BAN Río Grande in Tierra del Fuego province, after their deployment there in early May. Two of the squadron's pilots, Capt Zubrizarreta and Lt Marquez were killed during the Falklands conflict.

of the two Mirages was naive, as it left the rear aircraft exposed. Sure enough, Barton swung around onto its tail and launched a Sidewinder. Lt Carlos Perona didn't see it coming – the first he knew was when his aircraft blew apart. This, then, was the first aircraft shot down by a Fleet Air Arm fighter since the Korean War. The pilot ejected though, and landed in the water just off the coast of West Falkland. Perona made it safely ashore. His flight leader, Capt Garcia Cuerva, was less fortunate.

Thomas came in behind the remaining Mirage and launched a Sidewinder, just as Cuerva dived into a layer of cloud. The Fleet Air Arm pilot never saw it strike, and the attack was written off as a possible kill. In fact, the Mirage had been badly damaged, and Cuerva limped off towards Port Stanley, with fuel streaming from his ruptured tanks. When Cuerva reached the airfield, he was fired at by its AA guns; his jet was shot down by his own side, and he was killed. Meanwhile, a flight of three Daggers slipped past the Sea Harriers, while flying at just 300ft. Covering them were two more Daggers of 'Fortin' flight. They spotted Thomas's Sea Harrier disappearing into the clouds to their left, but they flew past unobserved.

'Torro' flight was searching out the British fleet, and was close to the fuel limit when they spotted three warships to the east of Port Stanley: *Glamorgan*, *Arrow* and *Alacrity*. Each of the three 'Torro' Daggers carried two 250kg bombs, and on the order of the flight leader, Capt Norberto Dimeglio, they banked towards the British ships, with each aircraft targeting a different ship. All of their bombs missed, but Arrow was hit by 30mm cannon fire, leaving holes in her funnel and wounding a sailor. The British had been lucky. Their anti-aircraft fire proved ineffectual, largely because their proximity to land had prevented their radars from giving any warning of the attack.

Meanwhile, another dogfight was developing over Port Stanley. Flt Lt Bertie Penfold and Lt Martin Hale of 800 NAS had just taken over the CAP mission when they were attacked by two high-flying Daggers. The British jets were at 20,000ft, 13,000ft below the Daggers, which launched an Israeli-made Shafrir anti-aircraft missile at Hale. He saw the tell-tale trail

The airmen of 801 NAS, pictured on the flight deck of HMS *Invincible* at the end of hostilities. The bearded figure in the centre of the back row is the squadron's commanding officer, Cdr 'Sharkey' Ward. As in her sister squadron, 800 NAS, roughly two-thirds of the pilots were Fleet Air Arm, and a third were Royal Air Force.

The first dogfight, 1 May 1982

The first air-to-air clashes of the war came on Sunday 1 May. This was the first day the British carrier group came within range of the Falklands. The day began with a raid by an RAF Vulcan bomber, followed by a series of ground attack strikes by Sea Harriers on Port Stanley airfield, and on the airstrip at Goose Green. Inevitably, the Argentinians responded by launching sorties from Argentinian air bases, to locate and attack the British Task Force. The Argentinians thought a landing was taking place near Port Stanley, and so countering this was their priority. Mirage IIIEA fighters from Grupo 8 de Caza were used as escorts for these missions, but on the one occasion a clash was possible, it didn't take place, as the British Sea Harriers refused to be drawn into a high-altitude battle with the French-built fighters.

In mid-afternoon though, two Mirage IIIAs from Grupo 8 de Caza took off from Río Gallegos, flown by Capt Garcia Cuerva and First Lt Carlos Perona. They headed west in another attempt to draw the British fighters into battle on favourable terms. Earlier, Argentinian naval propeller-driven planes had been attacked near Pebble Island, so the two Argentinian pilots headed there, to confront the enemy. They were detected on radar by HMS *Glamorgan*, and two Combat Air Patrol (CAP) Sea Harriers were directed to intercept them. The Sea Harriers, flown by Flt Lt Paul Barton and Lt Steve Thomas of 801 Naval Air Squadron (NAS) detected the Argentinian jets on their own radars and altered course directly for them. This was the opening move in the first real dogfight of the air campaign.

EVENTS

1. 19.06. The two Mirage jets flown by Cuerva and Perona flying at 40,000ft were vectored towards the British CAP by air controllers in Port Stanley. Their intention was to draw the British on, then perform a scissors manoeuvre, before launching their Magic air-to-air missiles. At 19.06, both sides made radar contact at a range of approximately 16 to 17 miles.

2. Barton and Thomas flying at 12,000ft were also directed towards the enemy aircraft, by the air controller aboard the destroyer HMS *Glamorgan*. When radar contact was made, the closing rate between the two groups of aircraft was calculated at a mile every three seconds.

3. On Cuerva's order, the Mirages had begun a dive down from 40,000ft, to lure the British into range. They were flying in echelon, a mile apart. At approximately 19.08, visual sighting was made at a range of 8nm.

4. At a range of five miles, Cuerva and Perona released their drop tanks, to improve their jets' manoeuvrability. Thomas thought these were AAMs.

5. At 19.10, Thomas and Cuerva flew past each other, 100yds apart, and at approximately the same height, 12,000ft. Cuerva banked to port, to get behind Thomas' jet, so he could launch a Magic missile.

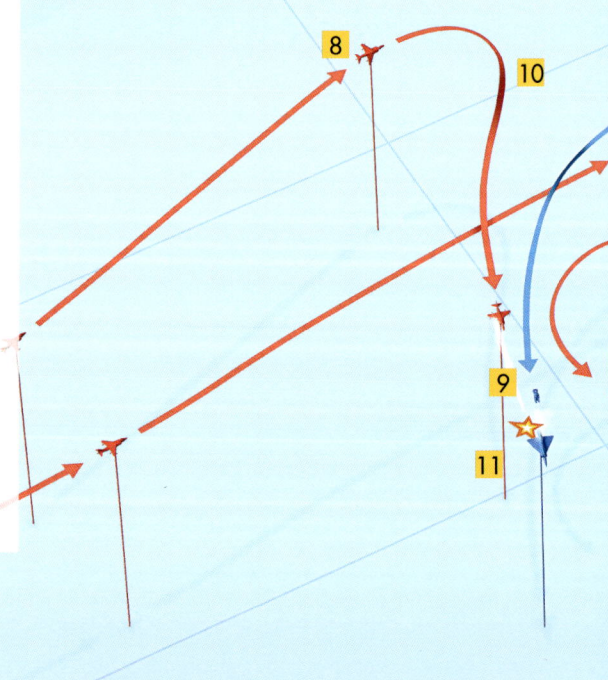

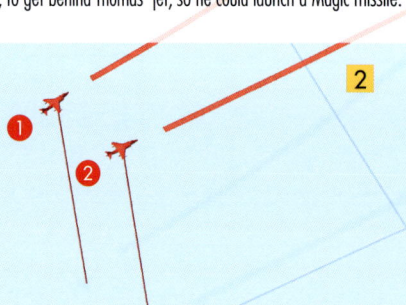

British: (801 NAS, from HMS *Invincible*) ●
1. Sea Harrier (Flt Lt Barton)
2. Sea Harrier (Lt Thomas)

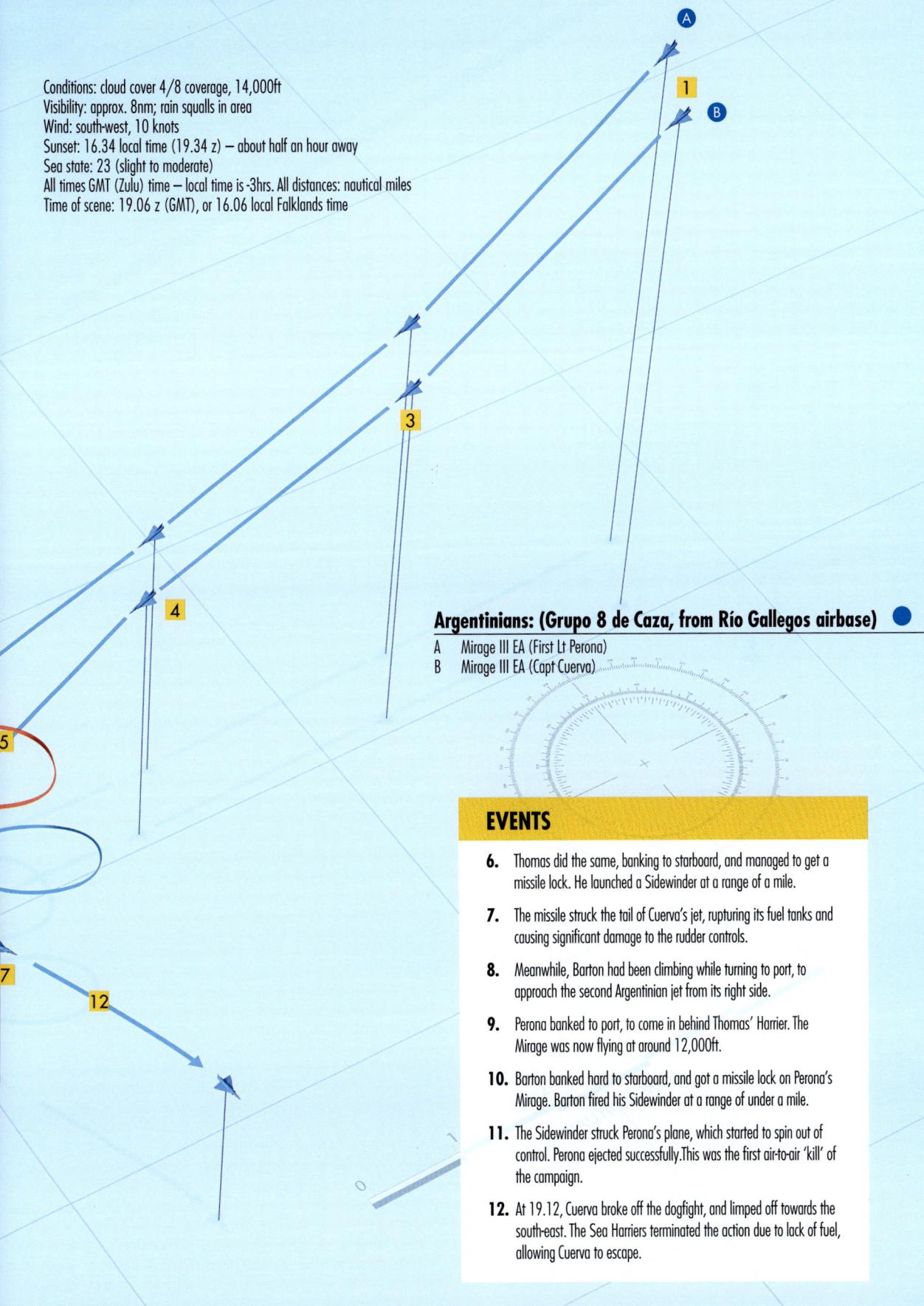

of the missile and took evasive action, and dropped chaff to confuse the missile's infrared homing system. The missile broke its targeting lock and plunged into the sea. Penfold had been watching this, and, climbing towards the Daggers, he launched a Sidewinder at extreme range. Miraculously, it struck the Dagger and brought it down. The pilot, Lt José Ardiles, was killed.

The last dogfight of the day came at dusk. An initial sortie by three Canberras of Grupo 2 in the late afternoon failed to find any British ships and returned to Trelew. A second flight then took off, led by Capt Alberto Baigorri. It headed towards a point 150 miles north of Port Stanley, as it was thought the British Task Force was in that area. The three two-man bombers were detected on radar by *Invincible*, and two CAP Sea Harriers of 801 NAS were sent to intercept them. Cdr Mike Broadwater and Lt Alan Curtis spotted the Canberras flying at sea level and dived into place behind them. Curtis launched a Sidewinder that hit one of the bombers, which crashed into the sea. Both the crew ejected. Broadwater tried to target the Argentinian flight leader, but the remaining two Canberras weaved, and Broadwater's missiles missed. The Canberras escaped, but Baigorri returned a little later, trying to locate his two downed crewmen. There was no sign of them, and they were never recovered.

That afternoon, the British Sea Harriers had their first confirmed 'kill', and a second 'possible kill'. In fact, after breaking off the fight, Cuerva headed to EAN Malvinas (Port Stanley airfield), to make an emergency landing. However, on his approach, he was shot down by the airfield's AA defences. Cuerva had survived the dogfight, only to be killed by 'friendly fire'.

As night fell, both sides had plenty to think about. During the first real clash of the war the Sea Harrier had proved its superiority over the FAA's Mirages and Daggers. No British aircraft had been lost, while two Mirages, a Dagger and a Canberra had been shot. The Vulcan strike and the subsequent Sea Harrier raid had also damaged Port Stanley airfield sufficiently to prevent its use by combat jets. The Vulcan attack demonstrated the reach of British land-based aircraft. As a result, the Mirages of Grupo 2 were withdrawn from the campaign and kept in reserve as interceptors, in case of Vulcan raids against the Argentinian mainland. As the Daggers were no real match for the Sea Harrier, they would be used primarily as bombers rather than fighters. Without the Grupo 2 Mirages, the Argentinians were now forced to concentrate on launching bombing strikes, rather than attempting to gain air superiority over the Falklands. This meant that after just one day of air combat, the Argentinians had ceded control of the skies to their opponents.

The weeks of attrition, 2–20 May

The Argentine Navy was still keen to make its mark. The carrier *Veinticinco de Mayo* put to sea with a screen of four destroyers and approached the TEZ from the north. Vice Admiral Lombardo's intent was to launch a strike against the British carriers using his air wing of eight Skyhawk A-4Qs, of the 3 Escuadrilla. Around midnight an S-2E Tracker aircraft detected the Task Force 150 miles north of Port Stanley. So, Lombardo ordered a dawn strike to be launched on Sunday 2 May. At 06.00 the carrier was 200 miles to the north-west of the British, but an unseasonal lack of wind made flying-off operations problematic: there wasn't enough wind over the flight deck to assist the bomb-laden Skyhawks to take off. So, the strike had to be aborted, and Lombardo ordered his carrier force to move closer to the coast, as he intended to try again when conditions were more favourable.

Meanwhile, another Argentinian naval force was at sea. The cruiser *General Belgrano* and its screen were off the Burdwood Bank, an undersea ridge to the south of the Falklands. Its escorts included two British-built Type 42 destroyers – *Santísima Trinidad* and *Hercules* – which were practically identical to their British counterparts. Soon after dawn on 2 May the radar emissions of *Hercules* were detected by a patrolling Sea Harrier of 801 NAS.

Sea Harriers ranged on the after deck of HMS *Hermes*. Sea Harriers '124', '127' and '123' pictured here were from 809 NAS, which arrived to reinforce the Carrier Battle group (CVBG) on 18 May. These aircraft were embarked in HMS *Hermes* and were attached to 800 NAS.

The nuclear submarine *Conqueror* then made contact with the Argentinian force and shadowed it as it maintained a patrol line south of the Burdwood Bank. This southern naval group was there to support Lombardo's attack on the British Task Force, but when this strike was cancelled the force centred around *Belgrano* remained in place, awaiting further orders. After urgent discussions in London, it was agreed that the *Belgrano* still posed a serious threat to the British Task Force. So, Cdr Chris Wreford-Brown of *Conqueror* was ordered to attack her.

At 14.57, *Conqueror* fired three 21in torpedoes, two of which struck the cruiser, blowing off her bow and holing her amidships. The *Belgrano* began listing heavily, and the order was given to abandon ship. The poor visibility and the lack of any distress signals meant that the cruiser's escorts were unaware of the disaster and steamed on. It was only after sunset that they returned to the scene and began rescuing survivors. In all, 323 Argentinian sailors died when the *Belgrano* sank. Afterwards, the sinking caused a political furore, as the *Belgrano* was outside the TEZ at the time she was torpedoed and steaming east. However, even her commander, Capt Hector Bonzo, later agreed that the sinking was a legitimate act of war.

That day though, a much more immediate threat to the Task Force was taking shape. Two Super Étendards of the 2 Escuadrilla based at Río Grande were armed with French-built Exocet anti-ship missiles, and took off that afternoon, to attack the British Task Force. Leading the strike was Capt Jorge Colombo. This target would normally have been beyond the reach of the Argentinian aircraft, but their range was to be extended by mid-air refuelling from a KC-130 Hercules tanker. That Sunday though, a technical problem meant that this couldn't happen, and so the mission was aborted. As this required re-programming the missile systems before the Exocets could be used again, this prevented a massed attack over the next few days, using all four operational Étendards.

That evening, two armed naval tugs headed north from Port Stanley to search for the two missing Canberra airmen, lost the previous evening. They were detected, and so early on 3 May two Lynx helicopters intercepted the two craft 60 miles north of Port Stanley. They then attacked using their Sea Skua anti-ship missiles. The tug *Comodoro Somellera* was sunk, while her consort *Alférez Sobral* was badly damaged. However, she managed to limp into an Argentinian port. The search for the missing airmen though, was never resumed.

The Type 42 destroyer HMS *Sheffield* was one of five warships in her class to serve in the Task Force. Arguably her crippling on 4 May by an Exocet strike was avoidable, if the ship had been more prepared to counter the threat posed by the air-launched anti-ship missiles. Her loss though, served as a wake-up call to the Task Force, which was more wary of this kind of attack.

The rest of Monday 3 May passed without any major incident. It seemed that the Argentinians were regrouping and reorganizing, and while the British CAP missions continued throughout the day, no contacts were made. That evening though, two Vulcans left Ascension Island on another *Black Buck* raid, accompanied by 11 Victor tankers. One of the Vulcans was a reserve aircraft, but it wasn't required. At dawn on Tuesday 4 May, Sqn Ldr John Reeve approach Port Stanley at low altitude and dropped 21 bombs over the airfield. None of them hit the runway.

As before, 800 NAS carried out a ground attack after the *Black Buck* attack, with three Sea Harriers led by Lt Cdr Gordon 'Gordy' Batt attacking Goose Green airfield. The Task Force was now to the south-east of the Falklands; this time the approach was from the direction of Choiseul Sound. While Batt and Lt Nick Taylor targeted the Pucarás parked on the apron using cluster bombs, Flt Lt Ted Ball was to drop a 1,000lb bomb on the grass runway after the first two aircraft had finished their attack. At 13.00, as Ball began his bombing run, he saw Taylor's Harrier struck by heavy-calibre fire, most likely from a radar-guided 35mm Oerlikon gun. The jet burst into flames, then crashed a short distance from the airfield, and Taylor was killed. Grim though this was for the British, things were about to get much worse.

At 07.10 that morning, an outlying warship in the British Task Force was detected by an Argentinian SP-2H Neptune maritime patrol aircraft of the navy's Escuadrón de Exploración. The navy's two ageing American-built aircraft were at the end of their operational life, and their electronic and radar systems were often faulty. On 15 May, they would be withdrawn from operations. On that Tuesday morning, though, the Neptune, piloted by Capt Ernesto Proni, demonstrated they still had value. Proni and his seven crew tracked the warship through the morning, while circling over the Burwood. Although the British detected the Neptune, they didn't consider it a threat. However, Proni had sent in a sighting report, and in response, at 07.30, two Super Étendards prepared to carry out another Exocet strike.

In all the Neptune detected four contacts, 60 miles to the east of his position. The assumption was that this was an outlying screen, protecting the carriers farther to the east. Weather conditions were poor, and visibility was often little more than half a mile. Still, as long as the Neptune kept tracking the British targets, the Super Étendards would be guided towards their target. At 09.45 Capt Augusto Bedacarratz and Lt Armando Mayora took off from Río Gallegos and headed east. Then, after refuelling from a KC-130 Hercules tanker, they dropped down to sea level, to avoid being detected on radar.

By 10.30 the two pilots could detect electronic activity 115 miles ahead of them. At the time the British Task Force was 85 miles south of Port Stanley, steering towards the south-west. *Hermes* and *Invincible* were each protected by a 'gatekeeper' – a Type 22 frigate whose Sea Wolf air defence missile provided close-range protection. Farther west were two screens of escorts, providing outer layers of protection. Then, 20 miles ahead of the carriers, a line of three Type 42 destroyers acted as radar pickets. *Coventry* in the north, *Glasgow* in the centre and *Sheffield* to the south were specialist air defence destroyers, and their Sea Dart missile systems were the Task Force's first line of defence. In addition, to the north-east, a pair of Sea Harriers were flying a CAP patrol and could be sent to intercept any attacker, if one was detected.

At 10.56, Bedacarratz ordered Mayora to join him as he climbed to 500ft, to see if they could locate the British fleet on their radars. They didn't, so the two jets dropped down to sea level again, flying at 500 knots, just 50ft above the sea. This pop-up though, was detected by *Glasgow*'s air-search radar, and the destroyer sent a warning to the other ships of the Task Force. Unfortunately, *Sheffield* was using her satellite communications system at the time, which blocked out certain radar frequencies. As a result, her own air-search radar was unable to detect the approaching aircraft. Then, at 10.58, the two Super Étendards climbed again, for another detection. This time their radar revealed two contacts, 20 miles ahead. These were *Sheffield* and *Glasgow*. As the southern radar contact appeared larger, Bedacarratz selected it as their target, hoping it was a carrier.

Glasgow sent out another urgent warning as her radar continued to track the approaching aircraft. By now though, it was too late to call in the CAP Sea Harriers. On *Sheffield* though, there was no immediate response to the warning, and her radar had still not detected the jets, which were now just 12 miles away. Then, at 11.02, Bedacarratz launched his Exocet, followed a couple of seconds later by Mayora. The Argentinian jets then banked and headed back towards Río Grande. The Exocets dropped down to sea level, and, after homing in on their target, they headed towards *Sheffield*, at a speed of just over 700 knots. Spotting them, *Glasgow* launched chaff, which was designed to confuse the missile's guidance systems. *Sheffield* though, did not.

At 11.04, the bridge crew of *Sheffield* spotted the sea-skimming missiles streaking towards them, and someone snatched the ship's broadcast microphone, and yelled the message "Missile

The French-built Dassault-Breuget Super Étendard strike aircraft of 2 Escuadrilla de Caza y Ataque were used by the Argentinian Navy to carry Exocet anti-ship missiles, one per aircraft, under the starboard wing. On 4 May, the aircraft in the bottom left was flown by Capt de Corbeta Augusto Bedacarratz during the attack on HMS *Sheffield*.

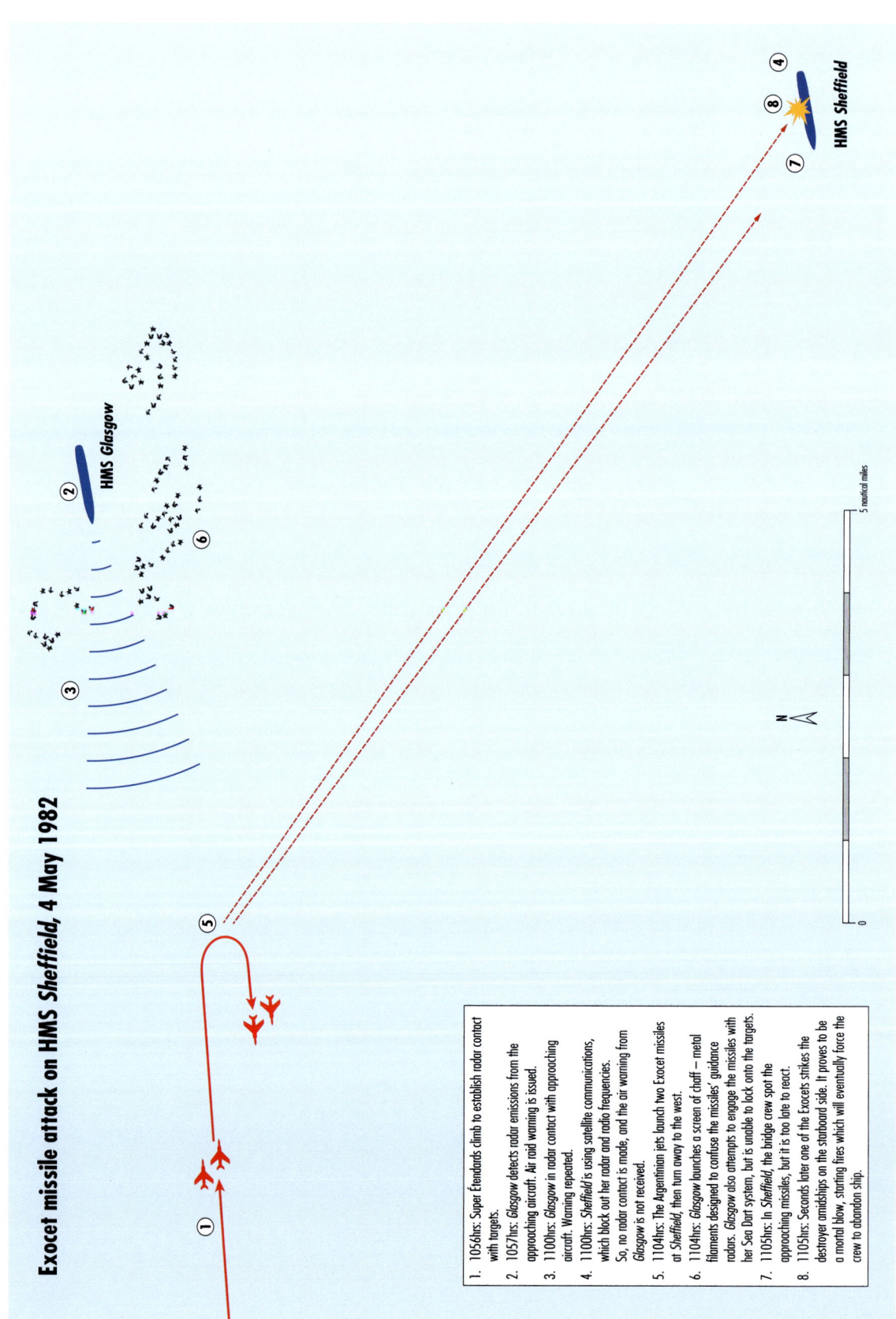

OPPOSITE EXOCET MISSILE ATTACK ON HMS *SHEFFIELD*, 4 MAY 1982

On the morning of 4 May, the British Task Force was to the south-east of the Falklands, while the carriers launched raids on Argentinian airfields. A forward screen of three Type 42 destroyers had been stationed 20 miles ahead of the carriers, to provide early warning of any attack, and to act as an air-defence shield. That morning though, two low-flying Super Étendards of the Argentinian navy got within 12 miles of this forward screen without being detected. At 11.04 (local time) they each launched an Exocet missile, then turned away to the west. The sea-skimming anti-ship missiles headed straight for the southernmost of the three destroyers, HMS *Sheffield*. The crew only had a minute to react before the missiles struck.

attack! Hit the deck!" Seconds later, an Exocet slammed into the destroyer's starboard side. It struck the ship amidships, just above the waterline, exploding in her machinery spaces. A fire erupted and spread rapidly. Meanwhile, the second Exocet streaked past the ship and plunged into the sea beside the Type 12 frigate *Yarmouth*. Its guidance system might well have been thrown off by *Glasgow*'s chaff. However, one Exocet was enough to doom *Sheffield*. As the Argentinian jets raced for home, smoke filled *Sheffield*'s compartments, forcing the crew to abandon both the bridge and the operations room.

Capt Sam Salt, who'd raced to the ops room from his cabin when the alarm was raised, was ultimately unable to save his ship. Several of *Sheffield*'s crew died in the attempt, as firefighting parties struggled to prevent the spread of the blaze. The frigates *Arrow* and *Yarmouth* came alongside to help fight the fire, but in the end all they could really do was help take off the crew. At 14.50 Capt Salt ordered his men to abandon ship. He and his senior officers were taken to *Hermes*, where they reported directly to R Adm Woodward. Salt had done all he could, but at the time Woodward exclaimed that 'someone has been bloody careless'. In the end though, it was, like many disasters, the result of a chain of events which had left *Sheffield* defenceless at the critical moment. Later, attempts were made to control the fire, and *Sheffield* remained afloat until 10 May, when she foundered while under tow from *Yarmouth*. She was the first Royal Naval warship to be lost due to enemy action since the end of World War II. A total of 20 of her crew died as a result of the attack.

The two Super Étendards returned safely to Río Grande, and it was only later, when the news of the attack was broadcast on the BBC World Service, that the Argentinians realized it had been *Sheffield* that had been hit. Although this was an important victory, it was also something of a lost opportunity. Argentina only had five Exocet missiles, and before the fighting began, it had been decided that these would be used to attack the two British carriers. Now, two of the five missiles had been expended, and the carriers remained undamaged. However, because of the loss of *Sheffield*, Woodward ordered the Task Force to withdraw to the east, where his ships were less vulnerable to air attack. While this protected the carriers, it had an impact on air operations.

Exocet AM-39 anti-ship missile
Length: 19ft 8in (6m) Weight: 1,720lb (780 kg)
Warhead: 364lb (165 kg)
Guidance: Infra active radar homing
Speed: 620 knots (Mach 0.93) Attitude: Sea-skimming
Launch platform: Argentinian Super Étendard strike fighter

An FMA IA-58 Pucará (A-529) of the Grupo 3 de Ataque, destroyed during the attack on EAN Calderon (the airstrip on Pebble Island) during the SAS raid there on 15 May. This was one of 6 Pucarás wrecked during the raid, together with 4 naval T-34 Mentor prop-planes and a Skyvan cargo plane.

The arming of a Sea Harrier during the campaign. These jets had four under-wing pylons, and a fourth mounting point under the centreline of the fuselage. There were also two attachment pods for gun pods, to augment the regular armament of two 30mm Aden cannon, fitted in pods under the fuselage.

Now, the Sea Harriers would be operating close to their extreme range, and so their patrol time over the Falklands would be reduced. Another result of the day's operations came from the loss of Lt Taylor's Sea Harrier over Goose Green. It was decided that no more low-level ground attack strikes would be made against well-defended targets. The British could not afford to lose many more Sea Harriers. So, from then on, attacks on ground targets would be carried out at a higher altitude, or from a distance, using the 'toss-bomb' method. Then, on 5 May the weather closed in, and increasingly rough seas, poor visibility and rain squalls greatly hampered air operations. For several days, these would largely be limited to performing CAP flights and reconnaissance missions.

Of course, the Argentinians were equally discomfited by the weather. For the Argentine Navy though, which was used to such conditions, there was a far more serious threat. It knew that British nuclear submarines were operating off the Argentinian coast. However, after the loss of the *Belgrano* this became a more immediate threat. As a result, it was decided to withdraw the Argentinian carrier to her base at Bahía Blanca, 700 miles to the north of the Falklands, where she would disembark her air wing. From then on, the fixed-wing aircraft of the navy would operate exclusively from land bases.

On 6 May the bad weather gripping the South Atlantic theatre cost the lives of two more pilots. At 09.00, a probable air contact was detected, near the burned-out hulk of *Sheffield*. So, two Sea Harriers of 801 NAS were dispatched to investigate. Lt Cdr John Eyton-Jones and Lt Al Curtis flew south to investigate but were never seen again. The likelihood is that the two jets collided in the poor visibility. This tragedy reduced the fixed-wing strength of the CVBG's air wing to just 17 aircraft. In the end, the contact was found to be a spurious one.

The poor weather continued, and while the CAP and reconnaissance patrols were flown, these were suspended on Saturday as conditions worsened. The weather improved slightly on

Sunday 9 May, so it was decided to launch a high-level bombing attack on Port Stanley. This would be a token operation, involving two Sea Harriers from 800 NAS flown by Lt Cdr 'Gordy' Batt and Flt Lt Dave Morgan. Each aircraft carried a single 1,000lb bomb. However, thick cloud cover over Port Stanley thwarted the mission, and the Harriers were recalled. As they withdrew though, Morgan detected a radar surface contact to the north. So, after confirming it wasn't a British vessel, Batt and Morgan set off to investigate.

It was the Argentinian intelligence-gathering trawler *Narwhal*, which the Harriers attacked and brought to a halt. *Narwhal* foundered the following day, while under tow. By Monday the Argentinians had also resumed flying operations, and a strike of two Skyhawks of Grupo 4 was sent to attack a bombardment force off Port Stanley, the destroyer *Coventry* and the frigate *Broadsword*. These Skyhawks though, were flying low, to avoid detection on radar, but the pilots misjudged their position. The jet flown by Lt Jorge Casco flew into a cliff on South Jason Island, at the north-west of West Falkland, and Casco was killed. His wingman, Lt Jorge Farias, was also lost, most probably after crashing into the sea. That afternoon, *Coventry* fired her Sea Dart at some unseen air contacts, possibly a C-130 tanker and her Mirage escorts, but no hits were scored.

The poor weather continued, and on Monday and Tuesday all operational flights by both sides ceased, apart from Argentinian maritime reconnaissance patrols, and British CAP missions. The rough sea conditions also led to the loss of *Sheffield*, being towed by *Yarmouth*. The intention was to take her to South Georgia, where she could be beached. Thanks to the rough seas though the flooding resumed. Eventually, *Yarmouth* had to cast the tow loose, and *Sheffield* rolled over and sank in a thousand fathoms of water, 90 miles south-east of Port Stanley.

Meanwhile, far to the north, eight Sea Harriers from 809 NAS and six RAF Harrier GR3s were gathering on Ascension, before being flown out to the SS *Atlantic Conveyor*, a container ship operated by the Cunard Line, which had been hastily converted into an aircraft transport. She also carried Wessex and Chinook helicopters, to be used by the British landing force, as well as fuel, ammunition and a myriad of stores, from aluminium sheets to make a temporary runway ashore to soap and toilet paper for the troops. She was expected to arrive in the TEZ around 20 May. Also heading south were naval reinforcements, supply ships, tankers, chartered civilian ships used as troop transports and hospital ships.

Weather conditions improved gradually on Wednesday 12 May, allowing both sides to renew active air operations. First into action were the Sea Harriers of 800 NAS. At 12.45 two

The Exocet attack on HMS *Sheffield*, 4 May 1982

On 4 May, the British Task Force was around 80 miles to the south-east of Port Stanley, as its two carriers conducted air operations over the Falkland Islands. They were protected by a ring of escorting warships, while some 20 miles to the west, a screen of three Type 42 destroyers formed an outer screen, a first line of defence. Their Sea Dart missile system would be the Task Force's first line of defence in the event of an air attack. Unknown to the British, the Task Force had been spotted that morning by an Argentinian Neptune maritime patrol aircraft, and two Argentinian Navy Super Étendard strike aircraft took off from Río Grande airbase, to launch a strike against this outer screen. Each strike aircraft carried an Exocet anti-ship missile, slung beneath its right wing.

After refuelling, Capt Augusto Bedacarratz and Lt Amando Mayora headed east towards the Task Force, flying just above the wave tops, to avoid being detected on radar. Visibility was poor, so they popped up twice, trying to locate the British ships on radar. On the second attempt, they spotted their targets – the line of three British ships – and at 11.04, first Bedacarratz in 3-A-202 and then Mayora in 3-A-203 launched their Exocets, some 20 miles away from the British ships. They then turned away, as the sea-skimming missiles dropped down and headed towards their targets. Minutes later, one of them struck the destroyer HMS *Sheffield*, the southernmost of the three British warships, and mortally wounded her, killing 20 of her crew, and wounding two dozen more. Six days later, *Sheffield* would founder while her charred hulk was being towed away from the area. The illustration shows the moment Bedacarratz launched his Exocet.

The aftermath of the hit on HMS *Sheffield* by an Exocet anti-ship missile on 4 May. It struck the destroyer amidships on the starboard side, damaging her machinery spaces and starting a fire which soon caught hold. Captain Sam Salt was left with no option but to abandon ship. Twenty of her crew were killed in the attack.

of them bombed Port Stanley airfield from 12,000ft, keeping out of range of the airfield's Roland SAM launchers. None of the four bombs hit the runway. At 13.40 another pair of 800 NAS Sea Harriers was approaching Port Stanley when they were ordered to abandon the mission. Four enemy jets had been detected, approaching from the west. So, as the Harriers were carrying bombs rather than Sidewinders, they would be useless in a dogfight. So, they returned to the carrier.

The four jets were Skyhawks, which had been detected on radar by the frigate *Brilliant*, as they crossed Falkland Sound. At the time *Brilliant* was to the east of Port Stanley, acting as 'gatekeeper' to *Glasgow*, which was carrying out a bombardment of the airfield. Over the past few days it had become regular British practice to carry out these bombardments. Now, though, with the skies clearing, the FAA could finally do something about it. So, at 13.00 four Skyhawks of Grupo 5's 'Cuna' flight took off from Río Gallegos, while four more from 'Oro' flight followed them half an hour later. Each Skyhawk carried either two 250kg bombs or a single 1,000lb bomb.

There would be no in-flight refuelling for this mission, so the aircraft would be at the very limit of their fuel when they reached Port Stanley. First Lt Oscar Bustos, leading 'Cuna' flight, spotted the warships at 13.38 as he passed over Port Stanley, and he ordered his flight to attack in pairs. *Glasgow* and *Brilliant* had already detected the attackers on radar when they were 50 miles away, and so they were ready. The first pair of Skyhawks flown by Bustos and his wingman Lt Jorge Ibarlucea dropped down to sea level and approached from the west. It appeared they were targeting *Glasgow*. Then, at 13.44, *Brilliant* launched two Sea Wolf anti-aircraft missiles, at a range of 5 miles. The fast-moving SAM missiles hit the two Skyhawks, which both exploded in mid-air, killing Bustos and Ibarlucea.

The second pair of Skyhawks was already committed by this stage, and Lt Mario Nivoli and Alverez Jorge Vázquez also headed towards *Glasgow*. On board the destroyer, the Sea Dart chose that moment to malfunction. So, it was up to *Brilliant* to save the day. The frigate's Sea Wolf launched again; Nivoli must have spotted the missile approaching just before impact, and he dived to avoid it. His low-flying Skyhawk crashed into the sea, and Nivoli was killed. The remaining Skyhawk gamely continued its attack, and Vázquez released his two 250kg bombs. They missed *Glasgow*, and Nivoli weaved away and made his escape. So, thanks to *Brilliant*'s Sea Wolf, three Skyhawks had been shot down. However, it was now the turn of 'Oro' flight, which had just made landfall over West Falkland.

The four Skyhawks sighted the two warships at 14.10 and dropped down to sea level. This time, all four jets would attack simultaneously. While Lt Juan Arrarás attacked *Brilliant*, Capt Antonio Zelaya, First Lt Fausto Gavazzi and Jun Lt Alferez Dellepiane targeted *Glasgow*. At the time the two British ships were steering towards the south-south-east, with *Glasgow* in the lead. Arrarás was fortunate. *Brilliant*'s Sea Wolf tracking system malfunctioned at the critical moment, and the frigate's only defence was from her 40mm Bofors guns and from small arms. Arrarás's two 250kg bombs missed, bouncing on the water and leaping over the frigate to land in the sea beyond her.

Meanwhile, *Glasgow* was still having problems with her Sea Dart, which left the destroyer with just the single 4.5in Mark 8 gun and her 20mm Oerlikons, backed up by small-arms fire. As Zelaya recalled: 'A few kilometres before we reached the target, they began firing at us. I didn't see any missiles, but I could hear the explosions of the anti-aircraft shells. As I neared the bomb-release point I concentrated my whole attention on the target. The sight of her huge radar scanner, continually rotating, remains etched in my memory.' The bombs dropped by Zelaya and Dellepiane missed the ship, but Gavazzi saw his 1,000lb bomb strike *Glasgow* amidships, near the waterline. He didn't see it explode though, as he raced away after his three companions.

His bomb didn't explode. It smashed through the unarmoured hull of the ship, only to pass out of it again on the port side. Only one crewman was wounded in the attack. However, the Argentinian bomb had still caused holes in her hull, just above the waterline; in anything other than a calm sea, *Glasgow* would take on water. So, she was withdrawn from operations, and later that day, another Type 42 destroyer, *Cardiff*, was ordered south from Gibraltar, to take her place. The man who'd dropped the bomb though, didn't live to celebrate his success. Lt Gavazzi's Skyhawk was shot down by ground fire from Goose Green during his return flight, and he was killed.

It had been a costly day for Grupo 5, losing four Skyhawks and pilots, while the plane flown by Vázquez was damaged as it landed back at Río Grande. The shortcomings of the American-supplied Mark 83 1,000lb bombs had yet to be evaluated, but the fact Gavazzi's bomb didn't explode should have caused concern. The Royal Navy though, had not only lost the use of a second Type 42 air defence destroyer, but the attack had also highlighted problems with both Sea Dart and Sea Wolf. The Type 909 fire-control radar serving Sea

A Skyhawk A-4Q of the Argentinian Navy's 3 Escuadrilla de Caza y Ataque, landing on the flight deck of the carrier ARA *Veintecinco de Mayo* during the early stages of the conflict. The carrier carried eight of these ageing but still effective strike aircraft.

An A-4B Skyhawk of the Grupo 4 de Caza, pictured while refuelling from a KC-130 aircraft. The ability to refuel in mid-air en route to the Falklands greatly extended the limited range of these aircraft, allowing them to strike British warships which would otherwise be beyond their operational reach.

Dart was hard pressed to detect low-flying targets. The Argentinians, having two Type 42s of their own, conveniently sold to them five years before, were aware of this shortcoming and had briefed their Skyhawk pilots accordingly. As a result of the damage to *Glasgow*, R Adm Woodward called a halt to daytime naval bombardment missions.

Then the weather closed in again, and on 13 and 14 May flying was impossible. So, the Argentinians were grounded, and even the British didn't fly CAP missions or ground-attack strikes. That Wednesday even another *Black Buck* operation was cancelled due to strong headwinds over the South Atlantic. There was a slight easing on Thursday forenoon though, although not over the Argentinian coast. So, at least the British could launch ground-attack strikes. Two days before, aerial reconnaissance had shown that the Argentinian garrison had been filling in the holes in the runway. Now, C-130 Hercules transports could now operate there with care.

So, when two CAP aircraft of 801 NAS took off from *Invincible*, each jet carried a single 1,000lb bomb. This was then used to 'toss-bomb' the runway from 15,000ft. While this was inaccurate, it demoralized the defenders, and there was always a risk of inflicting real damage. Once the bombs were dropped, the aircraft then resumed their CAP duties. That evening, as the weather deteriorated again, two Sea Kings from *Hermes*' 846 NAS landed a party of SAS troops on Pebble Island, where there was a small Argentinian airstrip. Aided by new night-vision equipment, the raiders planted demolition charges in several aircraft and withdrew without loss. As a result, the Argentinians lost six Pucarás, four T-34 Mentors and a Skyvan cargo plane. To cover the withdrawal, HMS *Glamorgan* bombarded the airfield, which added to the chaos.

Then the bad weather returned, and Friday 15 May was marked by low cloud cover. This prevented more photo-reconnaissance flights, which included examining potential amphibious landing sites. This was particularly frustrating, as the planning of the amphibious invasion was now well advanced, and it was expected to begin in less than a week. However, a Nimrod operating from Ascension managed to reach the Argentinian coast, and, using its powerful Searchwater radar, it confirmed that the Navy wasn't at sea.

Ironically, on the same day, the last working Argentinian Neptune maritime patrol aircraft was retired due to mechanical fatigue. That left the Argentinians without any long-range maritime reconnaissance capability. To make up the deficit, a Boeing 707 was used instead, ranging out into the South Atlantic, to detect British reinforcements heading towards the Falklands. On the afternoon of 15 May one of them located the ships carrying 3 Commando Bde, and the *Atlantic Conveyor*, which at the time was to the east of Buenos Aires. Incidentally, a second group of transports, including the SS *Queen Elizabeth 2*, was also at sea, and en route to Ascension.

That Friday afternoon conditions improved enough for British CAP missions to be resumed. The 801 NAS Sea Harriers flying CAP missions from *Invincible* 'toss-bombed' Port Stanley airfield, dropping seven 1,000lb bombs from 15,000ft. These, though, caused no real damage. 800 NAS also played its part, dropping six air-burst cluster bombs over the airfield that afternoon. This though, wasn't enough to prevent an Argentinian C-130 Hercules from landing that evening, bringing fuel and a runway repair detachment. It was also carrying a stripped-down 155mm howitzer. The Argentinians planned to emplace it to the east of the airfield, overlooking the coast, so it could fire on any British bombardment force that returned to the area. Over the next few days more guns would follow.

The general improvement in the weather on Saturday 16 May prompted the resumption of CAP flights as well as photo-reconnaissance flights. The main objective was the study of potential amphibious landing sites, but that Saturday morning, when the film was examined aboard *Hermes*, it revealed an Argentinian supply ship, the *Bahía Buen Suceso* alongside the pier in Fox Bay, on the south-west side of West Falkland. Another supply ship, the *Río Carcaraña*, was seen at Port King, on the East Falkland side of Falkland Sound. So, two pairs of 801 NAS Sea Harriers were sent to attack the two vessels. At 13.25 Lt Cdr 'Gordy' Batt and Lt Andy McHarg reached Port King, where they attacked the *Río Carcaraña*, which was set ablaze and abandoned. Then at 14.20 Lt Cdr Andy Auld and Lt Simon Hargreaves struck the *Bahía Buen Suceso*, which was raked by cannon fire and badly damaged. Apart from some minor bullet damage to the tail of Hargreaves' plane, the attack was unopposed.

Sea Harriers ranged on deck aboard HMS *Hermes*. The old carrier was the ideal platform for these jets, as she was larger than *Invincible*, and so could embark more aircraft, while also having the space for a substantial force of Sea King ASW helicopters.

On the night of 16–17 May, *Glamorgan* was sent inshore again, this time to bombard the southern coast of East Falkland, near Port Stanley, Darwin and Fitzroy. By now the amphibious landing site had been selected – San Carlos Water, an inlet on the north-eastern side of Falkland Sound and on the north-west coast of East Falkland. *Glamorgan* with her four 4.5in guns was therefore playing a part in a deception. The aim was to convince the Argentinians that the landing would take place to the south of Port Stanley. The newly emplaced Argentinian 155mm guns fired back but never managed to hit the old, but still-powerful, County-class destroyer.

Improved weather conditions encouraged the Super Étendards of 2 Escuadrilla to make another attempt at the British carriers on Sunday 17 May. The withdrawal of the Neptunes made this a tough prospect, but by analysing the movement of Sea Harriers detected by the air-search radar near Port Stanley, naval intelligence analysts were able to gain a rough idea of where the British carriers might be. It was decided to launch two Exocet-armed Super Étendards on the afternoon of 17 May, using KC-130H Hercules tankers to extend their range well to the east of the Falklands. Once in the likely area, the jets would fly at sea level, before popping up to locate a target using their own radar. In the end though, no sign of the British Task Force was found, and the aircraft returned to base. The Argentinians still had five Exocets, and the Super Étendard pilots were eager to use them.

The approach of *Atlantic Conveyor* early on 17 May was a major relief to R Adm Woodward. The 14 Sea Harriers and Harrier GR3s aboard would bolster his air wing's losses and greatly increase its fighting potential. That day, the aircraft were readied aboard *Atlantic Conveyor*, then sent south to rendezvous with the British carriers. To achieve this, 809 NAS was split into two detachments, with four of its Sea Harriers being sent to each carrier. The six Harrier GR3s of RAF No. 1 (Fighter) Squadron all embarked in *Hermes*. These RAF pilots had all undergone fast-tracked training in carrier operations, and their aircraft had been converted so they could operate alongside the Sea Harriers.

However, as 809 NAS didn't arrive with its own engineers, it meant the servicing teams on both carriers would be undermanned. Still, the arrival of *Atlantic Conveyor*'s reinforcements brought the embarked fixed-wing strength of the carriers up to 15 Sea Harriers and six GR3s in *Hermes*, and ten Sea Harriers in *Invincible* – a total operational strength of 31 aircraft. This was over a third more than had been embarked in the CVBG when it first arrived in

HMS *Hermes* was the last remaining carrier of the Centaur class, and was actually laid down during World War II. She went through several versions after she was commissioned in 1953, but in 1980–81, she was fitted with the 'ski jump' ramp seen here, to facilitate the operation of Sea Harriers, as well as Sea King anti-submarine helicopters.

the South Atlantic. As well as the arrival of 3 Commando Bde, the reinforcements included three Fleet Auxiliaries which carried much-needed stores and fuel. Even more welcome was the RFA supply ship *Fort Austin*, with four Lynx helicopters embarked, which had been fitted with hurriedly developed electronic decoy equipment, designed to confuse the homing systems of Exocet missiles. Two of these specially modified Lynxes were sent to *Hermes*, and another one to *Invincible*.

The newly arrived force also included the County-class destroyer *Antrim*, the Type 21 frigate *Ardent*, the Leander-class frigate *Argonaut* which carried Sea Wolf, and the older Type 12 frigate *Plymouth*. Now, Woodward felt he had the strength he needed to properly support the amphibious landing, which was scheduled to begin in three days' time. As the store ships joined the fleet, the business of transferring stores, men and equipment continued throughout Monday and Tuesday, as the Task Force remained well to the east of the Falklands, at the very eastern edge of the TEZ. During one of these transfers though, a bird strike led to the loss of a Sea King helicopter of 846 NAS. This resulted in the death of 22 men, many of whom were members of the SAS.

During this period before the landing a somewhat bizarre clandestine operation broke the routine of the preparations. Late on 17 May, *Invincible* – accompanied by *Brilliant* acting as 'gatekeeper' – sped west and approached the coast of Tierra del Fuego, Argentina's southernmost province. A Sea King helicopter from 846 NAS then flew in and landed an SAS team on Argentinian soil, some distance from the air base at Río Grande. The carrier and her escort then sped back to rejoin the Task Force before dawn. Meanwhile, the Sea King flew across the border into neighbouring Chile, where it was destroyed near Punta Arenas by her three-man crew. On 18 May the airmen surrendered to the Chilean authorities and were eventually repatriated. The official story was that the helicopter had crash-landed after being lost in thick fog.

The SAS group was eventually recovered without loss by the Porpoise-class diesel submarine *Walrus*, although the boat did strike an uncharted submerged rock during the recovery operation. The purpose of this clandestine mission, codenamed Operation *Mikado*, was to destroy the Exocet-armed Super Étendards based at Río Grande. However, the operation was hastily planned, without all the relevant intelligence information, and was widely regarded as a suicide mission. In the end, what forced Operation *Mikado* to be abandoned was the loss of surprise, as the helicopter had been detected as it crossed the coast. It was probably just as well, as several battalions of Argentinian troops were stationed around Río Grande, and so the chance of success was slim.

Meanwhile, at noon on 20 May, the newly arrived RAF Harrier GR3s had their first baptism of fire. As the weather cleared, three RAF Harriers took off from *Hermes*, and headed west towards Fox Bay, where the supply ship *Bahía Buen Suceso* had been attacked four days before. This time, the target was an Argentinian fuel depot. Wing Cdr Peter Squire led the strike, accompanied by Sqn Ldr Bob Iveson and Sqn Ldr Jerry Pook. The Harriers made landfall over the north-eastern coast of West Falkland. They then headed south across the sparsely inhabited island before making their final approach from the north-west, flying in a 'V' formation.

As Iveson recalled, 'We swept in low over the hills, then suddenly in front of us was our target; rows of jerry cans and 40 gallon oil drums laid out carefully on the ground.' It was a perfect target for the pair of cluster bombs carried by each Harrier. Squire went in first at 12.00, followed by Iveson and then Pook, and the fuel depot was comprehensively destroyed. The jets then made their escape without a shot being fired and had landed back on *Hermes* by 12.45.

Meanwhile, the British were making their final preparations for the amphibious landing. A final attempt at negotiations in the UN had broken down on 19 May, and so the British government had authorized the deployment of ground troops, to bring the conflict to a

OPPOSITE SAN CARLOS WATER

conclusion. Now, with the plans in place, everything depended on the weather. This though, was improving, and conditions were expected to remain favourable for the next few days. So, the landing, codenamed Operation *Sutton*, would go ahead as planned.

For the last few weeks the British had enforced a highly effective naval blockade of the Argentinian coast, using their nuclear-powered attack submarines. While some supplies had reached the Argentinian garrison in the Falklands by air, they had been denied the reinforcements and support they needed to strengthen their hold on the islands. However, although the Argentine Air Force and naval air units had been active since 1 May, they had not been deployed in strength. The likelihood, then, was that they had been saving their air assets for a full-scale counter-attack, as soon as the British attempted a landing. This meant that the ultimate test for both sides still lay ahead.

San Carlos Water

During the morning of 20 May the Amphibious Landing Group left the Carrier Battle Group and steamed towards the northern end of Falkland Sound, the north–south channel that divided the Falklands in two. The landing site was San Carlos Water, an inlet of the sound

On the starboard side of the 'ski jump' at the forward end of *Invincible*'s flight deck can be seen a ready-to-use area for ordnance, highlighting the range of bombs, pods, drop tanks and other fittings provided for the embarked Sea Harriers.

During the landing at San Carlos on 21 May, the type 21 frigate HMS *Ardent* was given arguably the most dangerous mission of the day – the defence of the southern approach to the landing site, over the Sussex Mountains to the south. So, Cdr Alan West (now Lord West) and his men were deployed on their own in Grantham Sound, where they were exposed to a string of Argentinian air attacks.

4½ miles from its northern end, and on its eastern side. Its entrance was a little over a mile wide, with Fanning Head to the north and Chanco Point to the south. When it reached the mile-long Fanning Island, the inlet divided, with one leg heading east to the settlement of Port San Carlos, at the mouth of the small San Carlos River, while the other leg, San Carlos Water proper, was a little over 5 miles wide and a mile across, with the scattered San Carlos settlement on its eastern shore.

This would be the main beachhead. For the navy, the two features which made it ideal as an amphibious landing site were the deep water there, and the fact that the hills on its eastern and western sides offered some protection from Argentinian air strikes. Effectively, the attackers had to approach the transport ships from along the length of San Carlos Water. Inevitably, in the days that followed, it would be dubbed 'Bomb Alley'. The same feature, though, was also a drawback. There was no effective radar warning to be had in San Carlos Water. So, a screen of warships had to be stationed around it, near Fanning Island, and farther out in Falkland Sound. Warships were also needed to form an anti-submarine screen in the sound, in case of underwater attacks.

Arguably the most exposed position was Grantham Sound, to the south-west of the landing beaches, and separated from them by a dog-legged ridge of high ground. A warship was needed to be stationed there to provide radar coverage near the southern end of San Carlos Water. That dangerous task was given to the Type 21 frigate *Ardent*. Then, around the entrance to San Carlos Water, *Broadsword* and *Plymouth* covered the northern end of 'Bomb Alley', while farther west in Falkland Sound, *Antrim*, *Argonaut*, *Brilliant* and *Yarmouth* provided additional cover, where their air-search radars could offer some warning of approaching air attacks. The force approached San Carlos in anti-aircraft formation, with the precious amphibious landing force ringed by warships. That morning it was grey and overcast, with patches of mist, a strong north-westerly wind and a lumpy sea. An RAF Nimrod maritime patrol aircraft from 206 Sqn flew overhead and soon confirmed that no Argentinian warships were at sea that morning. So, the only real threat would come from the air.

During the night of 20–21 May, while Sea Kings swept Falkland Sound for enemy submarines, *Antrim* and *Ardent* conducted a bombardment of Fanning Head, at the entrance to San Carlos Water. They then did the same around Choiseul Sound, on the southern side of East Falkland. This second bombardment was essentially a diversion. As another diversion, during the night an SAS team was landed near Goose Green, to pin down the Argentinian troops there. An SBS reconnaissance party was also landed near Fanning Head, to deal with a small Argentinian force, and while it was taken by surprise and forced to retreat, the Argentinians managed to shoot down two Commando brigade Gazelle helicopters, killing three men.

By 02.30 though, on Thursday 21 May, the stage was set for the main landing. The assault ships HMS *Fearless* and HMS *Intrepid* disgorged their landing craft and, covered by the guns of *Plymouth*, the men of 40 Commando and 2nd Battalion, Parachute Regiment (2 PARA) landed near San Carlos settlement. They were soon followed by 45 Commando. Argentinian opposition was minimal, as most of the garrison in the area withdrew. By dawn the British bridgehead was secure. Now, it was a matter of waiting for the inevitable Argentinian response. This though, would be helped by the weather. The grey misty conditions of the previous day and evening had gone and were replaced by clear skies. As Cdr Alan West of *Ardent* noted, 'When dawn came it was crystal clear. Once I saw the weather I knew we were in for a tough fight.'

Unsurprisingly, the Argentinian response began with local, Falkland-based aircraft, sent up to discover what was going on. The first of these was a low-flying Pucará of Grupo 3, piloted by Capt Jorge Benitez. It was one of eight Pucarás based at Goose Green that were still operational, and part of a two-plane patrol. Benitez though, was shot down at 07.55 by a hand-held Stinger SAM, launched by the SAS group. He had no warning of the missile, but he managed to eject and walked back to his base at Goose Green. By then, there was another form of protection available to the British. From sunrise, at around 06.30 on the 21st, regular hour-long CAP patrols of two Sea Harriers each were launched from *Hermes* and *Invincible*. The CVBG though, was well to the west of San Carlos, to avoid Argentinian attention.

This meant that when the Sea Harriers arrived over the beachhead, the aircraft only had limited supplies of fuel, and so loitering time in the patrol area was down to around ten minutes. So, pairs of Harriers on CAP missions were launched regularly, to relieve those on patrol. It was a thin enough CAP screen if the Argentinians launched a massed attack, and it was clear that the FAA had been conserving its strength for this moment. So, other Sea Harriers were held in reserve, so they could be scrambled at short notice if required. That morning they would be.

The CAP patrol area formed a large north-south rectangle, starting at Pebble Island, then running south, down through West Falkland to just above Fox Bay. It then extended east over Falkland Sound, then up to the north past San Carlos Water to Cape Dolphin, at the

On 21 May, while supporting the landings at San Carlos, the frigate HMS *Ardent* was attacked repeatedly by successive waves of Argentinian Skyhawks and Daggers. Three bombs struck her hangar and machinery spaces, which left the ship powerless. She was then hit again by several more bombs, and Cdr West ordered his crew to abandon ship. *Ardent* sank the following morning. In all, 22 of her crew were lost.

north-western tip of East Falkland. From there it extended back to the west to close off the rectangle over Pebble Island. The standard height for the CAP patrols was 8,000ft, but over West Falkland this was reduced considerably, to allow the ambushing of Argentinian aircraft approaching from the west, using the hills for cover.

The newly arrived RAF Harrier GR3s of No. 1 Sqn weren't used for these air defence patrols. They were primarily ground-attack aircraft, a role they continued to specialize in during the Falklands campaign. That morning the six-Harrier RAF squadron was tasked to fly reconnaissance flights over the landing area, and to support the ground troops if requested. That meant they were usually sent up with a payload of cluster bombs. The first two bomb-armed GR3s took off from *Hermes* at 07.00, to fly a reconnaissance sweep around the bridgehead. The bombs weren't needed though, no Argentinian activity was seen, and the two Harriers returned to their carrier. At 08.15 two more were launched, but one of them soon had to turn back due to landing gear problems. So, the remaining Harrier pressed on alone.

Its orders that morning were to conduct a low-level photo reconnaissance of Port Howard, on the West Falkland side of Falkland Sound, to see if its garrison posed any threat to the British landing. There, on its second pass, Flt Lt Jeff Glover's Harrier was fired on by an Argentinian Blowpipe hand-held SAM, and at 08.40 his aircraft was brought down. Glover ejected and landed in the water off Port Howard. Argentinian troops from Port Howard used a rowing boat to rescue him, and he was taken prisoner. Glover was eventually taken to Comodoro Rivadavia on the Argentinian mainland and was finally released on 8 July.

Meanwhile, two more Harrier GR3s left *Hermes* at 07.50 in response to a request from an SAS team on Mount Kent, which overlooked Port Stanley airfield. This time the target was Argentinian helicopters, which could be used to airlift troops to help contain the bridgehead. At 08.15 Sqn Ldr Jerry Pook and Flt Lt Mark Hare strafed a group of Argentinian helicopters on the ground. Although their first pass missed the target, Hare described the effects of the second pass: 'I saw my exploding rounds walking along the ground towards the helicopter. When I saw them exploding on it, I held my sight there, then it blew up with a spurt of flame and I pulled away.' By the end of the attack, two Argentinian Pumas and a Chinook had been destroyed. Hare's Harrier took three bullet hits, but it didn't prevent him from returning safely to the carrier.

An Argentinian Dagger of Grupo 6, pictured on 24 May during a low-level attack run up San Carlos Water, aptly named 'Bomb Alley' by the British. In the background is the RFA *Stromness*, a fleet stores ship, which had disembarked the Royal Marines of 45 Commando. The bow of the vessel in the foreground belong to the tanker RFA *Tidepool*.

The initial reconnaissance flights by the Pucarás based at Goose Green should have been followed by determined air attacks by the handful of MB-339s of 1 Escuadrilla based at Port Stanley. These should, after all, have been the first layer of response to the invasion, attacking the invasion force before the FAA was able to send strike aircraft over from the Argentinian mainland. On the morning of 21 May though, the response from Port Stanley was lacklustre. The previous day, a two-aircraft reconnaissance had been planned of San Carlos Water, as this was where Argentinian intelligence thought a British landing might be attempted. One of the two MB-339s though proved to be unserviceable, and so only one aircraft took off that morning, shortly before 08.15.

Lt Guillermo Crippa found the sun's glare made observation difficult, so he looped round slightly to the north, and approached San Carlos Water at 500ft, with the sun behind him.

A Dagger of Grupo 6, photographed during a bombing run over San Carlos Water on 24 May. Below her is the RFA *Sir Belvedere*, a Round Table-class landing ship, which survived a bomb hit which glanced off her midships crane, then passed on over the bulwark into the sea, without exploding.

Dogfight over West Falkland, 21 May 1982

On 21 May the British Amphibious Force began landing at San Carlos, on the western coast of East Falkland, some 50 miles west of Port Stanley. The Argentinians reacted by launching a series of air attacks on the British warships which were attempting to protect the landings. Inevitably, Sea Harriers from the British carriers were ordered to intercept waves of Argentinian aircraft, heading towards San Carlos from the Argentinian mainland. That afternoon, Cdr 'Sharkey' Ward and Lt Steve Thomas of 801 NAS were ordered to establish a patrol line over West Falkland near Port Howard, 30 miles west of the landing beaches. At 14.40, they spotted three Argentinian Dagger fighter-bombers flying east over the barren island, heading towards the beachhead.

The Daggers were flying at low level, to avoid detection on radar. So, the two British pilots dived down to intercept. Spotting Ward, Ratón flight leader Capt Guillermo Donadille ordered the aircraft to ditch their bombs and spare fuel tanks, and try to escape. By then though, Ward in Sea Harrier 004 had threaded between two of them, before turning hard to pursue them. Thomas in Sea Harrier 009 hadn't been spotted by the Dagger pilots, and he launched a Sidewinder, which brought down Lt Sena, flying Dagger C-407. Donadille in C-403 tried to climb into the clouds to escape, but Thomas pursued him and fired his second missile. It struck the Dagger's port wing, bringing it down. Meanwhile, the third Dagger, C-404, flown by Maj Gustavo Piuma shot at an unsuspecting Ward as he dived past him, but Ward turned, dived, and brought Piuma down with a Sidewinder.

In the illustration, Ward in the foreground is firing at Piuma, who is trying to bank away at low level, while in the background Thomas' second Sidewinder has just hit Donadille's Dagger. The smoking wreck of Sena's Dagger can be seen on the left. Amazingly, all three Argentinian pilots managed to eject, and lived to tell the tale.

Damage control teams battle a fire in the bows of the Batch II Leander-class frigate HMS *Argonaut*, after the ship was attacked in Falkland Sound on 21 May. The real damage though, came from two bomb hits aft, which killed two crew, and left the ship without propulsive power. The weapons seen here are her forward Seacat launcher, and her four Exocet anti-ship missile launchers.

He was rewarded with the sight of a British warship in the northern part of Falkland Sound. He saw a Lynx helicopter ahead of him and decided to fire at it. Then at 08.45, as he was busily approaching the Lynx, he spotted a British frigate off Fanning Head, to his right. It was the Leander-class frigate HMS *Argonaut*. So, the courageous Crippa ignored the helicopter and strafed the frigate instead, using his 30mm cannon. He also fired four unguided rockets at the warship for good measure, which wounded three of her crew, and caused light damage to her upperworks.

By then Crippa was rewarded with a sight of what he later described as 'the entire British fleet' arrayed beyond him, in San Carlos Water. He'd spotted the Amphibious Landing Group. Crippa turned away, having expended all his ammunition on *Argonaut*. He made his escape while trying to count the ships and dodging fire from the British warships. Crippa made it safely back to Port Stanley, and quickly reported what he'd seen. Minutes later, word of his discovery was radioed to Argentina. He would later be decorated for his courageous actions that morning.

In fact, the first strike aircraft from the Argentinian mainland were already on their way. Earlier that morning, unconfirmed sightings from land-based observation posts had reached FAA headquarters, which reported British warships in Falkland Sound. So, an order was passed to Grupo 6 de Caza to investigate. So, at 08.30, before any confirmed sighting reports from the Goose Green FAA Pucarás or Lt Crippa's naval MB-339 had raised the alarm, bomb-armed Daggers were on their way towards Falkland Sound. Six Daggers were dispatched from San Julián, although rather than operating as a formation, these headed east in pairs. Meanwhile, six more Daggers took off from Río Grande airbase, divided into two flights ('Nandu' and 'Perro'), each of three aircraft.

Meanwhile, around 08.30 a pair of Pucarás of 3 Grupo took off from Goose Green, in response to the British bombardment of the airfield and reports of British helicopters operating around San Carlos. They soon came under small-arms fire from the ground, and then were fired at by a Stinger SAM launcher, operated by the SAS troops deployed to the north of Goose Green. Following a request from the airfield, the two Argentinian pilots then launched a rocket attack against a British observation post near their airfield, before withdrawing back to Goose Green. That morning their airfield was a dangerous place, as the frigate *Ardent*, some 122 miles away in Grantham Sound, had been firing her 4.5in Mark 6

The last moments of the Type 21-class frigate HMS *Antelope*, which sank in San Carlos Water on 24 May, after burning through the night, following the detonation of two bombs lodged in her, which exploded during attempts to defuse them. The assault landing ship HMS *Intrepid* can be seen in the background.

gun at the airfield, and damaging a Pucará parked on the airfield's grass apron. Still, the small airfield remained operational and would fly other missions later that day.

The Grupo 6 Daggers from Río Grande took off in pairs, with lengthy intervals between departures. So, 'Cuna' flight was the first to appear over Falkland Sound, approaching from the north-west at around 10.40. Each carried two 250kg bombs. Cpt Norberto Dimeglio and Lt Carlos Castillo both headed towards the largest warship they could see, which looked as if it was isolated slightly from the others. It was the County-class destroyer HMS *Antrim*. The destroyer's crew were caught off guard, and the ship didn't respond to the threat, apart from with small-arms fire. Dimeglio and Castillo fired too, using their cannon to pepper the ship as they streaked towards her at sea level. The bombs though, all missed, and after climbing and banking, the Daggers headed home. For the crew of *Antrim*, it would be the start of a very trying day.

The six Daggers from Río Grande would be the next of these FAA formations to arrive. During the last leg of the flight towards West Falkland, its two flights reformed into two waves, with one wave half a mile behind the other. The whole formation was led by Major Carlos Martinez, who also commanded 'Nandu' flight. They had been guided towards their objective by a patrolling Argentinian Learjet, which was acting as a pathfinder that morning. It and the similar aircraft which relieved it would help guide the FAA air units towards their target throughout the day. After making

Commander Nigel 'Sharkey' Ward commanded 801 NAS during the Falklands conflict, the squadron embarked in HMS *Invincible*. He flew over 60 missions during the conflict, and achieved three confirmed 'kills', and participated in several more actions which resulted in the downing of Argentinian aircraft. This photograph though, taken during the conflict, reveals something of the tiredness and strain that accompanied the pressure of continuous combat air operations.

landfall over West Falkland, the two flights separated, taking diverging routes towards their target. Martinez led his leading flight of three Daggers over the northern portion of the island, flying low, before passing over Mount Rosalie at its north-eastern tip, to emerge at the northern end of Falkland Sound.

'Napo' flight was made up of Martinez and his two wingmen, Capt Carlos Rohde and Lt Pedro Bean. Martinez spotted the cluster of shipping in San Carlos Water and correctly assumed that this was the site of the amphibious landing. Other warships which were now shooting at him were also scattered in Falkland Sound. He decided to attack these scattered warships – the closest to him. These were HMS *Argonaut*, then off Fanning Head; HMS *Broadsword*, a little to the south off Chanco Point; and the larger HMS *Antrim*, a few miles farther south of *Broadsword*. Martinez selected *Broadsword*, while ordering his other two pilots to concentrate on *Argonaut*. A few seconds behind him, Capt Carlos Moreno, Capt Roberto Janett and Lt Héctor Volponi of 'Perro' flight were aiming for *Antrim*.

Each of the jets carried two American-produced 1,000lb bombs. *Argonaut*, which had just been hit by Crippa's rocket attack half an hour earlier, was more fortunate this time, as Bean's bombs missed the frigate. *Argonaut* fired with her Bofors guns and small arms, and she even launched an antiquated Seacat missile at her assailant. This was credited with the hit on Bean's Dagger, which brought it down over the sound. A far more likely candidate though, was a Sea Wolf missile launched from *Broadsword*. Although Bean was seen to eject, his body was never found. Martinez strafed *Broadsword* as he approached her across Falkland Sound, and although his two bombs missed, the frigate was hit by 29 30mm cannon rounds, which peppered her flight deck, wounded 14 crewmen, and damaged the two Lynx helicopters ranged on it.

Although Rohde should have attacked *Argonaut*, it seems he turned to the right and headed towards *Antrim* instead, a few minutes ahead of Cpt Moreno's 'Perro' flight. The large County-class destroyer was close to Cat Island, to the south-east of Chanco Point. It seems the old destroyer fired an immense and aged Sea Slug missile at the fast-approaching jet, but it failed to lock onto the target. Rohde was more accurate though, and like Martinez he strafed the destroyer as he sea-skimmed towards it. After climbing, at the last moment he released his 1,000lb bombs. One of them missed, but the other struck *Antrim*'s flight deck and then skidded over its after end to land on her after deck, next to the Sea Slug launcher. It continued through the anti-flash doors of the Sea Slug magazine, wrecking two of the

One of the most iconic and horrifying images of the Falklands conflict – the explosion of the Sea Cat magazine aboard HMS *Antelope*, during the evening of 23 May. An unexploded bomb detonated during an attempt to defuse it, killing and wounding the two-man disposal team. Fires raged, and the order was eventually given by Cdr Nick Tobin to abandon ship. The last crewman left just minutes before the magazine exploded and the ship became a burning pyre that blazed throughout the night.

The County-class guided missile destroyer HMS *Antrim* was nearing the end of her operational life when she was sent to the South Atlantic, but she was still a powerful warship, and a large one – similar in size to a World War II-era light cruiser. Unlike her sister ship HMS *Glamorgan*, she had only one twin 4·5in gun turret – 'B' turret had been replaced by four Exocet launchers.

18ft long missiles, then lodged itself in the after seamen's heads, or toilets. The bomb didn't explode, but a couple of small fires were started, which were quickly extinguished. The only casualties were two lightly wounded seamen, injured by flying metal fragments. It was a close call for Capt Brian Young and his crew.

This was the first direct bomb hit of the day. However, the three Daggers of 'Perro' flight were now only minutes away. In the interim, Young moved the damaged destroyer closer to *Broadsword*, whose modern Sea Wolf system could provide some extra protection, now that *Antrim*'s Sea Slug was proved to be so ineffective. At 09.43 'Perro' flight appeared over the cliffs of West Falkland, and surprisingly, despite the damage to the after deck, *Antrim* managed to fire off a Sea Slug towards the approaching Daggers, which had descended to just above sea level. This missile though, wasn't being fired offensively. Instead, Young had ordered it to be jettisoned, to reduce the risk of it exploding on its launcher. It made sense to launch it in the general direction of the enemy aircraft, even though there was no chance of it hitting anything other than the sea.

Antrim also mounted two Sea Cats, one on each side of her hangar. The port one, closest to the Daggers, had been damaged earlier and so was out of action. It seems her starboard one wasn't launched, as its arc of fire was blocked by the ship's superstructure. Still, everything else fired, from *Antrim*'s four 4·5in guns and 20mm Oerlikons to her crew armed with small arms, including GPMGs – the British Army's general-purpose machine gun. Surprisingly, two of the Daggers turned away, but the third, flown by Capt Janett, pressed home the attack, but his bombs missed the destroyer. However, Janett's 30mm rounds fired as he approached, wrecked the destroyer's Wessex 3 helicopter on her flight deck, started a fire, and injured seven crew, two of them seriously.

Another of the 'Perro' Daggers headed for the RFA *Fort Austin*, which was lying close to *Broadsword*, half a mile south of Chanco Point. The likelihood is that the pilot mis-identified the target and attacked the store ship rather than the two warships nearby. All that *Fort Austin* had to defend herself were small arms, and the crew braced themselves for the impact of the bombs. Then, when the Dagger was around 914m away to the west, it was hit by a missile and broke apart. The likelihood is that this was caused by a Sea Wolf launched from *Broadsword*, but this was never confirmed. However, the incident was filmed, and broadcast around the world.

The remaining Daggers turned south and escaped, being fired on by *Ardent* as they passed her to the west. Their escape though, wouldn't be entirely free of drama. HMS *Brilliant* had been tracking the raid. She was serving as the fighter direction ship for the Sea Harriers on CAP, and so these were alerted. Lt Cdr 'Fred' Frederiksen and Lt Martin Hale of 800 NAS turned to pursue the Daggers, but having dropped their bombs, the Argentinian jets were faster. As Hale described it, 'I dropped in behind the left-hand man in their formation and got a good missile lock. The range was a bit on the high side, but I decided to give it a try.' Sure enough, the Sidewinder didn't have the range, and it exploded some distance astern of its target. Running low on fuel, the two Sea Harriers then had to give up the chase, and the Argentinians headed for home.

Antrim limped away into the more sheltered entrance to San Carlos Water, where her crew treated their wounded and tried to repair the damage. The real problem, of course, was the unexploded 1,000lb bomb in her after heads, but a bomb disposal team were soon brought on board and began the task of defusing it. Everywhere else, as the Amphibious Landing Group continued to land stores and equipment, the battered ring of protective warships grimly waited for the next attack. Noon came and went without another attack. Minutes later though, two bomb-armed Pucarás appeared to the south of *Ardent* and dropped down to launch another attack.

The two bomb-armed Pucarás of Grupo 3 de Ataque took off from Goose Green at noon and turned towards the frigate in Grantham Sound, some 12 miles away to the north-west. The two jets were piloted by First Lt Juan Micheloud and Sn Lt (Major) Carlos Tomba, and each was armed with a pair of 250kg bombs. The Pucarás were spotted as they began their approach, flying in low from the south. *Ardent* was ready though, and her 4.5in gun opened up almost immediately, followed by her two 20mm Oerlikons and small-arms fire from rifles and GPMGs. The frigate even launched a wire-guided Seacat missile. Wisely then, Micheloud and Tomba felt the volume of fire was too great, and turned away. They headed back towards Goose Green. Capt West of *Ardent* wondered if this had been because of his frigate's firepower, or because the two Argentinian pilots realized that there were Sea Harriers patrolling in the area.

In fact, the two Pucarás had been detected by the air-search radar of HMS *Brilliant*, which was coordinating the operations of the Sea Harrier CAP screen, and the air direction officer had notified the CAP aircraft. Moments later the CAP Sea Harriers on patrol over Falkland Sound were banking towards the south to intercept the two Pucarás. Unusually, at that point there were three of them, rather than two, as the decision had been made to strengthen the CAP screen when possible, as heavier air attacks were expected during the afternoon. The Sea Harriers were flown by Cdr 'Sharkey' Ward and Lt Steve Thomas of 801 NAS, accompanied by Lt Cdr Alisdair Craig of newly arrived 809 NAS, fresh from *Atlantic Conveyor*.

It was Thomas who first spotted the two Pucarás, flying low towards Goose Green. Thomas and Ward both picked a target and dived into the attack. Unwilling to waste Sidewinders, the Fleet Air Arm pilots engaged the Pucarás with their 30mm cannon. Micheloud escaped from Thomas and then Craig by weaving at ground level, avoiding the bursts of fire aimed at him. He then flew through a narrow valley in Lafonia south of Goose Green, where the fast-moving jets were unable to get to grips with him. However, Ward caught up with Tomba and opened fire with his guns. His first burst went ahead of his target, so he lowered one of his flaps and tried again, flying at a few dozen feet over the ground.

Later, he described what followed: 'I wanted to get as low as possible behind the Pucará, and dropping the flap brought my nose and gun axis down relative to the wing line. Aiming … hotline on '' firing! The left engine of the Pucará now erupted into flame, and part of the rear cockpit canopy shattered.' Still, Tomba kept flying, trying to evade Ward, and it took a third burst to bring his aircraft down, as the wing was damaged, and the aircraft caught fire.

Tomba was forced to eject, and his aircraft crashed near Drone Hill, 10 miles south-west of Goose Green. Ultimately what saved Micheloud was the lack of fuel of the Sea Harriers, which forced them to return to their main CAP patrol. So, the Argentinian pilot managed to avoid his pursuers, and when it was reported the Sea Harriers had broken off, he returned safely to Goose Green. Like Benitez, the surprisingly uninjured Tomba eventually managed to walk back to his airfield.

That was the final contribution of the air wing of the *Guarnición Militar Malvinas* in that morning's activities. From that point on, it would be up to the far more effective fighter-bombers operating from the Argentinian mainland to stop the British amphibious invasion. The departure of the remaining Daggers from Río Grande had been delayed, so the next force to appear over Falkland Sound were Skyhawks from Grupo 5 based at Río Gallegos. The strike was planned to coincide with another attack by Grupo 4, but this didn't work out as planned. The Grupo 5 strike was made up of four of the light attack jets, led by Capt Pablo Carballo. They had rendezvoused with a KC-130 Hercules soon after taking off, but one of the Skyhawks was unable to refuel and so was forced to turn back. A second encountered problems drawing on the fuel in her drop tanks, and so also had to return to base. The remaining two continued though and flew over West Falkland to reach the sound beyond the island. There they spotted a large ship, and Carballo and his remaining wingman Jr Lt Leonardo Carmona began their bombing run.

Carballo though, quickly identified her as the wrecked supply ship *Río Carcaraña*, which had been attacked and abandoned five days before. He aborted the attack, but Carmona didn't get the message and continued his bombing run. His bombs missed though, and Carballo ordered his wingman to return home. He then banked and flew northwards up the coast of East Falkland, looking for another target. The first ship he encountered was *Ardent*, which was still at her post in Grantham Sound. Carballo dropped down to sea level and flew straight towards her. The approaching Skyhawk was spotted from *Ardent*'s bridge, but it was too late to open up with anything apart from the Oerlikons. The bombs straddled the frigate, but missed her. It was now 12.55. Carballo flew over *Ardent*'s mast, then banked around and headed away towards the south.

The foredeck of a British Type 42 destroyer. In the foreground is a fully-automatic 4.5in/Mark 8 gun mount, which was supported by a dedicated fire-control radar. Astern of it, in front of the bridge, is the ship's Sea Dart launcher, which mounted two of these long-range air defence missiles. Their limitation though, was their fire control radar's poor performance when tracking low-flying targets.

Up above, the CAP patrol was just about to be relieved, and Lt Cdrs Neil Thomas and Mike Blissett from 800 NAS were about to head back to *Hermes*. The fighter director in *Brilliant* had detected the Skyhawk on the frigate's radar and requested that Thomas and Blissett give chase. They dropped down to 1,500ft, just below the sparse clouds, and headed south down Falkland Sound. In the end, they didn't engage Carballo's Skyhawk, as at 13.00 a far more important target had appeared. Blissett explained, 'When we were about three miles east of Chartres Settlement I caught sight of four Skyhawks in front of me about 3½ miles away, flying across my nose from left to right. They had just crossed the coast on their way in.' The Skyhawks were from Grupo 4, and after taking off from San Julián they had refuelled successfully, before crossing the West Falkland coast near the tiny hamlet of Chartres. As soon as they spotted the Sea Harriers, the Skyhawks broke formation, jettisoned their bombs and drop tanks, and tried to escape towards the south.

Blissett described what followed: 'I was in the lead, with Neil on my left and about 400yd astern, with all of us in a tight turn. The Skyhawks were in a long echelon, spread out over about a mile. I locked a Sidewinder on one of the guys in the middle and fired.' Moments

A Sea Harrier FRS.1 aboard HMS *Invincible*. The aircraft were secured to the flight deck to prevent damage when the ship pitched and rolled, which also helped the flight deck teams arm and prepare the aircraft before she was moved to her take-off spot.

later Thomas fired too, his Sidewinder streaking past Blissett's port side. Then, at 13.04 Blissett's missile struck its target: 'Suddenly, about 800yds in front of me, there was a huge fireball, as the aircraft blew up in the air.' First Lt Daniel Manzotti was killed instantly. Moments later Thomas's Sidewinder struck another Skyhawk, which began cartwheeling towards the ground. This time, Lt Nestor Lopez was able to eject, although neither British pilot noticed it at the time. Blissett couldn't get a missile lock with his second Sidewinder, but he managed to fire a burst of cannon fire at a third Skyhawk before it weaved out of the way. With that, the two Sea Harriers broke off the fight, as they were running short of fuel, and returned to their carrier.

It was clear by now that the Argentinians were attempting to coordinate their strikes more effectively. By now their squadron leaders would have heard reports from the first wave of pilots and would plan their attacks accordingly. This was exactly why the CAP strength had just been increased from two to three aircraft. Still, that day the British first line of defence was the flight controller on board HMS *Brilliant*, supported by the frigate's Type 968 air-search radar. If Argentinian aircraft left it too late to duck down to sea level when approaching West Falkland, the approaching aircraft could be detected, and the patrolling CAP vectored towards them. That is precisely what happened next. Four Daggers from Grupo 6 had been detected as they approached the island's western coast, and the CAP patrol, Lt Cdr 'Fred' Frederiksen and Lt Andy George of 800 NAS, were sent to intercept them well before they reached Falkland Sound.

The original plan was for a coordinated Dagger strike, with six Daggers of 'Laucha' and 'Raton' flights from San Julián and six more of 'Cueca' and 'Libre' flights from Río Grande joining forces. They would then fly east in a large formation and so overwhelm the British CAP defences. In practice, however, it proved impossible to coordinate the attacks that precisely. 'Cueca' flight was made up of Capt Horacio González and his wingmen First Lt Hector Luna and Lt Juan Bernhardt, while 'Libre' was made up of just two Daggers, as one aircraft had to return to base. The two that remained were flown by Capt Amilcar Cimatti and Capt Higinio Robles. During the approach to West Falkland the Daggers from the two bases had been unable to rendezvous en route, and each flight also flew in its own formation. As a result, 'Cueca' flight was in the lead as it dropped down low, and after making landfall near Chartres Gonzalez turned towards the north-east, so he could enter Falkland Sound from its northern end.

At 14.16 Frederiksen sighted the three Daggers as they crossed over the island. With George following behind him, Frederiksen moved in behind 'Cueca' flight and targeted the left-hand Dagger. This was the jet flown by Luna. He recalled, 'We were about four miles from the target and flying very low... and at that moment I saw a Sea Harrier turning above me.' He tried to warn Gonzalez but couldn't get through. He then saw a second Harrier behind him, just as it fired its Sidewinder. It hit Luna's jet, which started to spiral towards the ground, and crashed near a hillside at 14.20. Luna ejected but was injured when he landed. By then Frederiksen had opened up on Gonzalez with his 30mm cannon, but the Argentinian broke left, while the Harrier banked to the right and shot at the third Dagger as it swept by. The Argentinians successfully broke contact though, but instead of running for home they came round again and headed east towards the British ships.

Meanwhile, 'Leo' and 'Orion' flights of six Skyhawks from Grupo 5 de Caza had managed to bypass the CAP patrol entirely and reached Falkland Sound without being attacked. The six jets had taken off from Río Gallegos, and without refuelling they bypassed West Falkland entirely, flying to the north of the island instead. Having flown low past Pebble Island, they then banked to the south and emerged without warning over Mount Rosalie, at the north end of the sound. The Grupo 5 Skyhawks then concentrated on the closest British ship, HMS *Argonaut*. Capt Kit Layman's frigate was busily launching a helicopter, evacuating the wounded from the morning attack by Lt Crippa's MB-339. Although taken by surprise, *Argonaut*'s crew opened up with Bofors and small-arms fire. They also launched at least one

On 4 May, the Type 42 destroyer HMS *Glasgow*, commanded by Capt Paul Hoddinot, detected the approaching Super Étendard strike that crippled *Sheffield*, but her warnings went unheeded. Eight days later, on 12 May, *Glasgow* and the Type 22 frigate HMS *Brilliant* formed a '42–22 combo', deployed east of Port Stanley to draw enemy aircraft. That day, *Glasgow* was hit and damaged by a bomb which failed to explode, but four Argentinian Skyhawks were lost.

Seacat. One of the Skyhawks may have been hit and shied away, but the others all reached the frigate and dropped their 1,000lb bombs. Two of them struck her at 14.30.

The first smashed through her hull at the waterline, between the engine room and boiler room, and caused extensive damage. The other also entered the frigate's hull near the waterline, rupturing fuel tanks and wrecking the ship's sonar before landing up in the Seacat magazine, where it set off two missiles and killed two crewmen. Surprisingly, neither bomb exploded. The frigate wasn't answering her helm and was heading at speed towards the rocks around Fanning Head. Fortunately, she was able to drop her anchor, and the frigate slewed to a stop. The quick-thinking officer, Sub-Lt Peter Morgan, who made that happen was awarded a medal.

It was just as well that the CVBG had increased the number of Sea Harriers deployed in a CAP role over Falkland Sound. It was clear that the air strikes were less piecemeal than before, and not only were attacks from the same *Grupo* being better coordinated, but the whole of the FAA effort that day was now centred around larger-scale attacks, involving different types of aircraft. So, there was a real danger that the British air defences would be overwhelmed. Sunset that day would come at around 16.02, and about 40 minutes after that it would be too dark to carry out attacks. That meant the Argentinians still had another two hours to deliver a knock-out blow on the Amphibious Landing Force and its escorts. The FAA and CANA were well aware of this and so were prepared to commit everything they could to the assault.

Once again it was *Ardent* which bore the brunt of the attacks. The two remaining Daggers of Grupo 6's dogfight over West Falkland attacked the frigate, and at 14.30 the two jets dropped a 1,000lb bomb apiece. The likelihood is that one of them missed the target, while the other struck the frigate but didn't explode. The details from both sides are contradictory. The timeline from *Ardent* though, suggests that the serious damage inflicted to her that afternoon was the result of an attack by a naval Skyhawk. The two Skyhawks approached from the south-west, having flown under the radar throughout their flight from the Argentinian mainland. Three A-4Q Skyhawks swept over the sound from the direction of Fox Bay, and the first British ship they saw was the already-damaged *Ardent*.

They made their approach from astern, and although Cdr West tried to turn, to allow his 4.5in gun to fire, there wasn't enough time. The Seacat launcher refused to work, which left the frigate with just her port-side 20mm Oerlikon and two GPMGs. The jets attacked in a line-astern formation, and at around 14.45 each Skyhawk dropped three 250kg 'Snakeye' bombs. Three of them hit the frigate, two detonating in her hangar, wrecking her Lynx helicopter and killing ten men. The third burst through the deck into her machinery spaces. It didn't explode but caused electrical problems, which *Ardent*'s damage-control parties tried to fix while also dealing with the carnage in the hangar.

Meanwhile, a few minutes earlier HMS *Brilliant* requested Lt Cdr 'Sharkey' Ward and Lt Steve Thomas to intercept three fast-moving radar contacts which had just made landfall over West Falkland. At the time, the two British pilots of 801 NAS had been flying in a circuit up and down a valley a few miles to the east of Port Howard. Moments later two low-flying Daggers ('Rótan' flight from San Julián) were spotted entering the western end of the valley, and the two Sea Harriers turned to intercept them. Ward threaded between the two enemy jets, then turned to starboard to come round onto their tail. The Argentinian pilots hadn't spotted Thomas, and he took up position behind the left-hand Dagger. He launched a Sidewinder at 14.40, which struck the Dagger flown by Lt Jorge Sena, bringing it down.

As Thomas lined up on the Argentinian flight leader, which was trying to climb into the low clouds, a little to the right Ward was shot at by a third Dagger, which he hadn't seen. The burst missed the Sea Harrier, but Ward banked and dived after it, as the Dagger tried to fly off just above the ground. By then Thomas had another lock on his target, and he launched his second missile. It caught Capt Guillermo Donadille's plane just as it reached the cloud layer, and it began spinning towards the ground. Seconds later, Ward did the same, bringing down the third Dagger flown by Maj Gustavo Piuma. Despite the low altitude, all three Argentinian pilots managed to eject successfully and were deposited on the valley floor, close to the wreckage of their aircraft.

Afterwards, Thomas was hit by ground fire while flying over Port Howard but managed to limp back to *Invincible*. This dogfight though, had occupied the two British pilots, and

An Argentinian Douglas A-4C Skyhawk attack aircraft of Grupo 4 de Caza, deployed at the civilian airport of San Julián in Argentina's Santa Cruz Province during the conflict. The Grupo 4 Skyhawks had a lighter camouflage colour than the aircraft in Grupo 5, based at Río Gallegos.

OPPOSITE
HMS *Broadsword*, pictured here, and her sister HMS *Brilliant* (F90), brand new Type 22 frigates, carried a pair of Sea Wolf close-range air defence missile systems apiece, mounted forward of the bridge and above the hangar. They tended to be used as 'gatekeepers', either protecting the British carriers, or paired up with Type 42 destroyers like HMS *Coventry* or HMS *Glasgow*, on detached operations.

so they didn't notice another Dagger flight slipping past them. The three Daggers reached Falkland Sound and carried out an attack, but failed to achieve any hits. As Ward began his own flight back to *Invincible*, he spotted three Skyhawks heading towards *Ardent*. Although he couldn't intervene, he called *Brilliant*, who directed his relief CAP team, Lt Clive 'Spaghetti' Morell and Flt Lt John Leeming, to attack them. These two fresh Sea Harriers dived towards the Skyhawks but couldn't intercept them before they dropped their bombs.

Lt Marcello Marquez must have seen Morell moving in behind him, as he turned away, only to be hit by a cannon burst from Leeming. Marquez was killed, and his jet plunged into the sea. It was now 15.11. Morell then lined up on the leading Skyhawk, flown by the flight leader, Capt Alberto Philippi, and having locked on, he launched a Sidewinder. Seconds later the missile struck the Skyhawk, bringing the plane down. That left Lt Jose Arca's Skyhawk. It had been damaged during the attack on *Ardent*, so he turned towards the east, hoping to reach the relative safety of Port Stanley. Morell banked towards this last Skyhawk, but his missile wouldn't lock onto the jinking target. So, he used his cannon again, and a well-aimed burst struck the Skyhawk, which was damaged, but continued to weave away.

Both Leeming and Morell had to give up the pursuit of the damaged jet as they were low on fuel, leaving Arca free to continue to Port Stanley, over 50 miles to the west, trailing smoke as he went. He tried to line up on the runway to make an emergency landing but discovered his undercarriage had been damaged. So, unable to make it home, he was forced to eject over the airfield, and his Skyhawk crashed nearby at 15.21. That ended the final dogfight of the day, and a black hour for the Argentinians, who had lost seven aircraft in the space of an hour. However, before they were lost, the three naval Skyhawks of 3 Escuadrilla had already dropped their bombs.

Both Philippi and Arca had scored hits, and two 250kg Redeye bombs had struck the after end of the frigate, killing several crewmen and wrecking the ship's steering gear. Cdr West coaxed *Ardent* inshore and dropped anchor, as *Yarmouth* came alongside to help. West gave the order to abandon ship, and the wrecked frigate was left to burn. She finally sank at dawn the following morning, 22nd May. In all, 22 of *Ardent*'s crew had been killed, and another 37 wounded. Still, despite the cost, the primary mission had succeeded. The troops of 3 Commando Bde had been safely established ashore. This meant the battle for the Falklands had now entered a new phase. From that point on, the primary aim of the CVBG was to support the troops ashore, and to prevent the Argentinian air and naval forces from interfering in the land battles to come.

The turning of the tide

The 21 May had been a decisive one for both sides. In the aerial fighting that day, the Argentinians had lost two Grupo 3 Pucarás, five Grupo 6 Daggers, and a total of five Skyhawks, two from Grupo 4 and the rest from the 3 Escuadrilla. Of these, nine had been shot down by Sea Harriers, one by a ship-launched missile, one by a land-based one, and the last by a combination of small-arms fire from a warship and the 30mm rounds from a Sea Harrier. In return, the British had lost one Harrier GR3, shot down by ground fire. No Harriers had been shot down by enemy aircraft, and during the day's fighting, they had ably proved their superiority over their Argentinian opponents. To balance this, though, *Ardent* had effectively been destroyed while *Antrim* and *Argonaut* had been seriously damaged, and *Brilliant* and *Broadsword* had suffered minor damage. In the confined waters of Falkland Sound, these modern warships had shown themselves to be dangerously vulnerable to air attack, especially where there was often little or no advance warning.

Dawn though, on Saturday 22 May revealed clear skies over San Carlos Water. Fortunately for the British, the Argentinian mainland was cocooned in low cloud, making flying

operations impossible. So, the British had a reprieve. Around San Carlos the British troops reinforced their beachhead, and supplies continued to be unloaded. However, this time the transport and supply ships didn't linger in the area and withdrew back out to sea after unloading. The British CAP was sent up at dawn, which came at 07.30, and Lt Cdr Fred Frederiksen and Lt Ian Hale of 800 NAS spotted an Argentinian patrol boat in Choiseul Sound, which led to Goose Green. The *Río Iguazu* was delivering supplies to the airfield, but it never made it. The boat was strafed by the two Sea Harriers, and was run aground and abandoned, while it blazed fiercely.

At noon, Sqn Ldr Jerry Pook led a four-Harrier strike on Goose Green, which the No. 1 Sqn aircraft attacked with cluster bombs. Despite heavy anti-aircraft fire, none of the attacking GR3s was hit. It was early evening before the sky cleared on the Argentinian mainland, and shortly after 16.00 two Skyhawks appeared, penetrated as far as San Carlos Water and dropped their ordnance. The bombs missed, and the pair returned to base. This, it seems, was more of an armed reconnaissance than anything else. It would though, offer a foretaste of what was to come the following day.

Sunday morning began harmlessly enough, with a dawn raid on the small airstrip at Dunnose Head, a settlement on the western side of West Falkland. It was thought it was used by Argentinian supply planes, so at 08.00 four Harriers from No. 1 Sqn bombed

On 25 May, the Type 42 destroyer HMS *Coventry* accompanied by the Type 22 frigate HMS *Broadsword* were deployed to the north of the Falklands, to act as a 'missile trap'. Essentially, they were there to ambush Argentinian aircraft heading towards San Carlos Water. Instead, it was the two British warships which were ambushed, and *Coventry* was sunk.

it. It turned out the airstrip was unused, but it was bombed anyway, causing damage to nearby buildings and wounding an islander. A little later, at 10.15, the CAP patrol spotted four Argentinian helicopters heading up Falkland Sound towards Port Howard. Flight Lt David Morgan of 800 NAS dived down to strafe the leading one, but when the helicopter, a Puma, tried to evade, it flew into the ground near Shag Cove and blew up. The other helicopters landed and were abandoned, where they were shot up on the ground by Morgan, and by his CAP replacements, Lt Cdr Tim Gedge and Lt Cdr Dave Braithwaite of 801 NAS. This though, was merely the prelude to what would be another busy day over Falkland Sound.

The first attack came at 14.00, a low-level bombing run by four Skyhawks of Grupo 5. This time their target was *Ardent*'s sister ship, the Type 21 frigate HMS *Antelope*. One of the pilots, Capt Alberto Philippi, was so low that his plane struck the frigate's mainmast as he flew over the ship, damaging its drop tank. One of the Skyhawks was shot down, either by a Sea Wolf from *Broadsword* or *Antelope*'s own Oerlikon. The plane struck the frigate's mast before crashing, and the pilot, Lt Luciano Guadagnini, was killed. This attack was closely followed by a strike by three naval Skyhawks from 3 Escuadrilla. During these attacks, at 14.09, *Antelope* was hit by two bombs, both of which failed to explode. The damaged frigate limped off into San Carlos Water, where a demolition team were embarked. By now, Rapier SAM launchers had been deployed around the bridgehead, and these were used during the attack. However, the operators found it hard to target the low-flying jets. One of the Skyhawks was badly damaged during the attack. Later, Lt Cdr Carlos Zubizarreta crashed while landing at Río Grande, and was killed.

This attack was followed by a lull, which lasted until 15.50 when three Daggers from Grupo 6 arrived with almost no warning and launched an unsuccessful attack. Ten minutes later, one of them was spotted by the CAP as it flew home over Pebble Island. Lt Cdr Auld and Lt Hale of 800 NAS turned towards it but found the faster jet was drawing out of range. Then, a second Dagger was spotted a few miles behind the first. This time Hale managed to work his way in behind it and launched a Sidewinder. It hit the tail of the Dagger, and it blew apart. The pilot, Lt Héctor Volponi, was killed instantly. That proved to be the last raid

This remarkable photograph was taken during a low-level bombing attack on HMS *Broadsword*, on 25 May. Two A-4B Skyhawks from Grupo 5 are pictured just seconds before they released their bombs during an attack on the frigate. One of these bombs struck her flight deck, and destroyed the frigate's Lynx helicopter. Minutes later *Broadsword*'s consort HMS *Coventry* was mortally wounded during a similar attack.

The SS *Atlantic Conveyor* was a container ship, which was hired by the British Ministry of Defence, and then converted into a makeshift aircraft transporter, complete with a flight deck. She was crippled by an Exocet missile on 25 May, and sank three days later. Twelve of her crew were killed, including her Master, Capt Ian North.

of the day, at least in Falkland Sound. That afternoon, two Super Étendards of 2 Escuadrilla took off from Río Grande, to reach the British carriers, to the north-east of the Falklands. However, they couldn't find the British, and after looping to the east of the archipelago they returned to base, still carrying their Exocets.

On board *Antelope* attempts by a two-man Royal Engineers team to defuse the two 1,000lb bombs continued through the afternoon. Then, without warning, one of the bombs detonated, killing one of the team and badly wounding the other. *Antelope* was badly damaged by the blast, and her keel was broken. Cdr Nick Tobin ordered his crew to abandon ship. This was done shortly before the resulting fire touched off the Seacat magazine, and the frigate burned fiercely through the night. What remained of *Antelope* broke apart and sank later the following day. It was a costly end to the day. Two men had been lost – one when the bomb struck, and the other when it exploded. To make this even worse, another Sea Harrier was lost that day, during an evening strike on Port Stanley airfield by four aircraft of 800 NAS. During the otherwise successful attack, Lt Cdr Gordon 'Gordy' Batt's plane was hit by ground fire, and it crashed within a mile of *Hermes*, as Batt tried to nurse it home, and he was killed. So, the Task Force had lost another warship, and another Sea Harrier. The landing at San Carlos, however successful though it was, came at a heavy price.

On the morning of Monday 24 May, 800 NAS launched another strike against the airfield, operating alongside No. 1 Sqn. The runway was hit by 1,000lb bombs, but no significant damage was caused. This though, was very much a sideshow now, as the real focus of action remained San Carlos Water. That morning, rather than risk more surprise strikes, the British had changed the way they operated. The destroyer *Coventry*, with the frigate *Broadsword* acting as 'gatekeeper', took up station north of Pebble Island. There, their radar should give them advance warning of Argentinian strikes. Then, by working with the CAP fighters, they had a chance of ambushing the attackers before they reached Falkland Sound.

The scheme worked perfectly. At 10.50 Lt Cdr Auld and Lt Dave Smith of 800 NAS were off Pebble Island when *Broadsword* reported enemy aircraft approaching from the west. The two Sea Harriers turned towards them and soon spotted four Daggers from Grupo 6, flying low. Coming in behind them, Auld got a missile lock and launched a Sidewinder.

Air attack on the Task Force, 25 May 1982

Tuesday 25 May was Argentina's National Day, the anniversary of the country's independence from Spain. The air force had already celebrated it that morning by the bombing and sinking of the Type 42 destroyer *Coventry*. The Argentinian naval air wing began its own strike late that afternoon, when two Super Étendard strike aircraft took off from Río Gallegos airbase, each carrying a single Exocet anti-ship missile. They flew northwards off the Argentine coast, to refuel in mid-air to the east of Puerto Deseado. The British didn't know that the Super Étendards had been adapted to allow mid-air refuelling, and so they mistakenly thought they were out of range of these Exocet-armed jets. R Adm Woodward and his Task Force were in for a surprise. After refuelling, the jets turned east over the South Atlantic, heading towards the probable position of the British Task Force, a location based on the prediction of Argentinian naval analysts. This proved fairly accurate. At that moment, the British were 60 miles north-east of Port Stanley.

When the two pilots detected the radar emissions of warships to the south-east, they turned their planes towards them. They made their approach flying at 550 knots, just above sea level, to avoid being spotted on radar. At 19.36 z (16.36 local time), the two jets climbed to 150m, to acquire a target on their own radar sets. This done, they launched their two Exocet missiles, at a range of 23 miles. Moments later the missiles were speeding towards their target, covering a mile every six seconds.

Royal Navy (Task Force)
1. HMS *Ambuscade* (Type 21 frigate) Cdr Mosse
2. SS *Atlantic Conveyor* (modified container ship) Capt North
3. HMS *Brilliant* (Type 22 frigate) Capt Coward
4. HMS *Hermes* (Centaur-class aircraft carrier) Capt Middleton (Flagship, R Adm Woodward)
5. RFA *Sir Tristram* (Round Table-class landing ship) Capt Green
6. HMS *Invincible* (Invincible-class light aircraft carrier) Capt Black

Argentinian Navy (2 Escuadrilla de Caza y Ataque)
A Super Étendard 203 (Capt Curilovic)
B Super Étendard 204 (Lt Barraza)

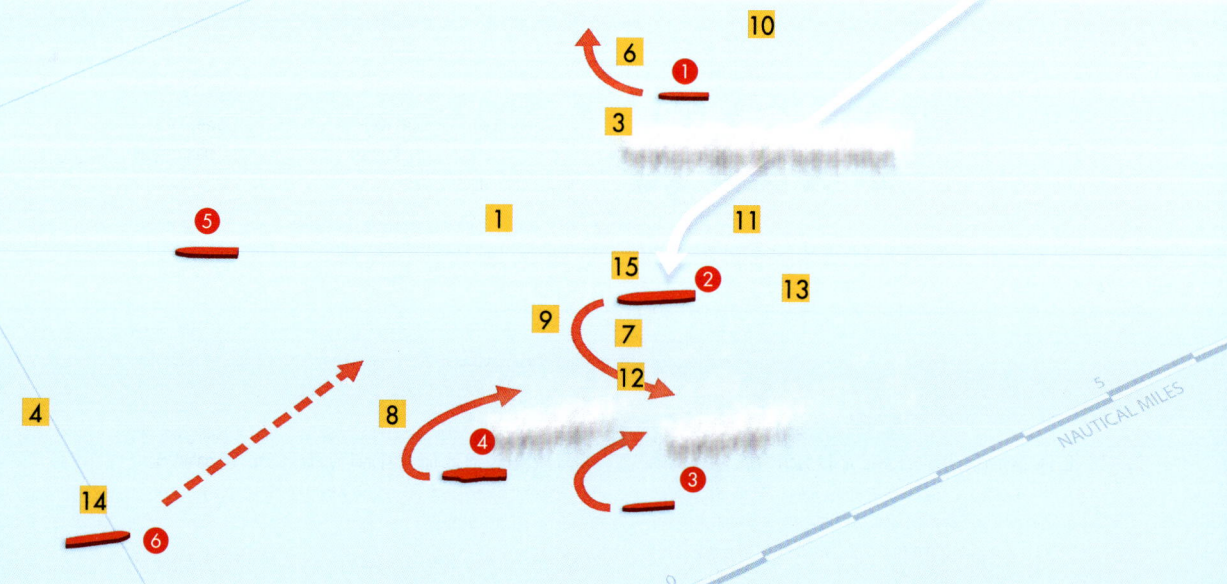

Conditions: cloud cover 5/8 coverage, 3,000–4,000ft
Visibility: approx. 5nm; rain squalls in area
Wind south-south-west, 24 knots
Sunset: 15.59 local time (19.59 z)
Sea state: 4–5 (moderate to rough)
All times GMT (Zulu) time – local time is -4 hours
Time of scene: 19.35 z (GMT), or 16.35 local Falklands time.

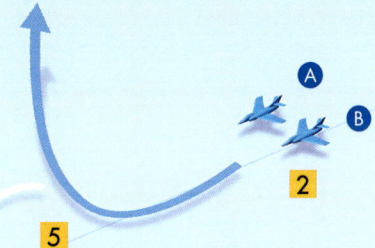
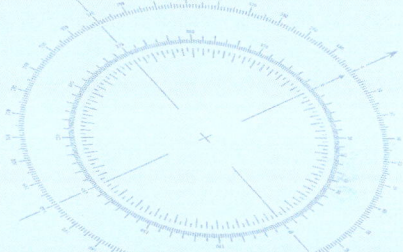

EVENTS

1. 19.35 (z) (15.35 local time). The British Carrier Battle Group (CVBG) is steaming towards the south, on a course of 170°, making 12 knots. To the east are two hired merchant supply ships, on the same course, while two Type 42 air-defence destroyers (*Exeter* and *Glasgow*) are deployed 20 miles from the carriers.

2. 19.36. Having detected British radar emissions to the south-east, two Super Étendards climb to 150m, to acquire the Task Force on radar. Once its location is established, the pilots prepare to launch their Exocet missiles.

3. 19.36. The frigate *Ambuscade* detects two approaching aircraft on her air-search radar, at a bearing of 310° and a range of 30 miles. An immediate air attack warning is broadcast to the Task Force.

4. 19.37. The destroyer *Exeter*, 20 miles to the south-west of the CVBG, also detects aircraft radars, 40 miles to the north. She too transmits a warning.

5. 19.39. The jets launch their Exocet, then bank away to starboard. The release point is 23 miles from the nearest British warship. The missiles target the largest of the three detected targets. At the time this is the carrier *Hermes*.

6. 19.39. 40s. *Ambuscade*, making 16 knots, turns to the north-west and launches chaff to distract the Exocets away from the CVBG.

7. 19.40. The air attack alarm is issued, and *Atlantic Conveyor* is ordered to turn 40° to port, to head away from the threat (on a new course of 130°). However, due to a signalling error, the container ship is ordered to turn to port onto a course of 040° instead. This places her side-on to the approaching missiles.

8. 19.40. 10s. The Task Force flagship (the carrier *Hermes*) has the largest radar signature in the fleet, making her the primary target. She is turned hard to starboard, heading directly towards the threat (new course 310°), with her bows pointing towards the approaching missiles to reduce her exposure. The destroyer *Brilliant* makes the same change. At this point *Hermes* and *Brilliant* launch chaff.

9. 19.40. 25s. *Atlantic Conveyor* sees the chaff launches by *Ambuscade* and *Hermes*, as the container vessel begins a hard circling turn to port.

10. 19.40. 55s. *Ambuscade* fires her 4.5in gun at the missiles, without success. Two sea-skimming Exocets pass astern, heading towards *Hermes*.

11. 19.41. At this point, as *Hermes* is bows-on to the missiles, *Atlantic Conveyor* appears the larger target. The missiles veer, away from *Hermes*, and towards *Atlantic Conveyor*, their sensors confirming the latter as the largest target.

12. 19.42. 10s. *Atlantic Conveyor* is still turning hard to port when one of the Exocets strikes her port quarter. The second missile probably crashes into the sea nearby. Neither missile is detonated.

13. 19.42. 30s. Most of the bridge crew are killed or injured, the vessel has lost all propulsive power, and is on fire amidships. The order is soon given to abandon ship.

14. 19.42. 30s. *Invincible* launches a Sea Dart at the departing aircraft, but they pass out of range before it reaches them. Helicopters are scrambled from around the Task Force, to go to the assistance of the stricken container ship.

15. SS *Atlantic Conveyor* finally sinks early on 28 May 1982. A total of 12 of her crew die, including her Master, Capt Ian North.

As the missile sped off, he saw the others break right and turned to follow them. His missile targeting system locked on again, and he fired his second missile. Both Sidewinders hit their targets, and the planes were brought down. Meanwhile, Smith had managed to shoot down a third jet with his own Sidewinder. With that, the remaining Dagger jettisoned its bombs and turned away, back to base. Two of the pilots, Major Luis Puga and Cap Rául Diaz managed to eject, but Lt Carlos Castillo was killed when his jet blew up. The two Sea Harriers chased the remaining Dagger, but it quickly drew out of range.

Meanwhile, other waves of attackers were approaching Falkland Sound and were undetected by *Coventry*, as they made their approach around the other, southern side of West Falkland. First, at 11.12 three Grupo 4 Skyhawks swept over Grantham Sound and reached the anchorage over the ridge in between, before diving down again to make their bombing run. The defenders were taken completely by surprise. At 11.14 their bombs hit three RFA landing ships. RFA *Sir Belvedere* was only hit by a glancing blow, but unexploded bombs lodged in RFA *Sir Galahad* and *Sir Lancelot*. Although the first was defused quickly, *Lancelot* was put out of action for a week, until a specialist team could defuse it.

After their bombing run, the Skyhawks then banked away, chased by Rapier missiles, 20mm Oerlikon rounds and small-arms fire. In the process, all three jets took hits by small-calibre weapons before they flew out of range. Then, four more Daggers appeared by the same route. Again, the Rapiers were launched at them, and small arms, but the jets swept on, almost in line abreast, and attacked the largest ship they could see, the store ship *Fort Austin*. The undamaged Daggers then turned west over the mouth of the inlet and sped away. The bombs all missed the supply ship, but it had been a close call. Still, one of the Skyhawks had been badly hit, and the plane crashed into the sea as it tried to limp back to base. Its pilot was unable to eject.

As for the Daggers, they too had been damaged during the attack, but they all made it back to base. Their other flight though, of four Daggers, was less fortunate. It was the one jumped by Auld and Smith over Pebble Island. Argentinian losses were heavy, both in aircraft and pilots, and the new phenomenon of damage from ground fire and warships merely added to the FAA's problems. However, during the day they'd noted the presence of *Coventry* and *Broadsword* and guessed the reason for their presence so far west. This, of course, also made them a potential target.

As 25th May was Argentina's National Day, the British considered it likely that this would encourage the Argentinians to launch a major attack. This prompted R Adm Woodward to move the CVBG closer to San Carlos, to reduce the range for his Sea Harriers. This now placed the two carriers 130 miles north-east of the beachhead. This allowed a stronger CAP presence, and this, combined with the early warning offered by *Coventry*, provided a stronger defence of the beachhead in the event of a massed air attack. In the end though, it turned out that the Argentinians had other plans.

That morning a reconnaissance Learjet flew over San Carlos at 40,000ft and returned with exact details of the British positions there. *Coventry* launched a Sea Dart at it, but the range was too great. This was followed from 12.20 on by flight-sized formations of Skyhawks from Grupos 4 and 5 attacking San Carlos Water from the south, after passing southwards around West Falkland. One of them, flown by Lt Ricardo Lucero, was shot down by fire from a combination of weaponry, but the pilot ejected safely. Another Skyhawk pilot, Cap Jorge Garcia, was less fortunate and failed to eject before his plane was shot down. Another Skyhawk from Grupo 5 was shot down by friendly fire while flying over Goose Green, and the pilot, Cap Hugo Palaver, was also killed. The British ships were undamaged. Around the same time, six Sea Harriers and GR3s launched another ground-attack strike on Port Stanley airfield, using their 'toss-bomb' technique, but no significant damage was caused.

Then, the Argentinians launched a well-planned attack on *Coventry* and *Broadsword*, which were still on radar picket patrol, 10 miles north of Pebble Island. Six A-4B Skyhawks of Grupo 5 led by Lt Cdr Ruben Zini took off from Río Gallegos, then refuelled from a waiting KC-130 Hercules tanker. Two of the jets though, developed problems and had to return to base. The remaining four then passed over West Falkland and were lost on British radar. However, instead of carrying on towards San Carlos they turned north, and at 15.19 they re-emerged over the sea at Pebble Island in two pairs, one a mile behind the other. Two Sea Harriers of 800 NAS were flying a CAP mission, but these were ordered out of the way by Capt David Hart-Dyke of *Coventry*, to avoid friendly fire from his missiles.

The first two Skyhawks began their bombing run at sea level, heading towards *Broadsword*. They were too low for Sea Dart to engage them, and at that critical moment the frigate's Sea Wolf fire-control system malfunctioned, leaving the British ships almost defenceless. At 15.24, Cap Marcus Carballo and Lt Carlos Rinke dropped four bombs and scored one hit. A 1,000lb bomb wrecked the frigate's flight deck and helicopter, before bouncing away into the sea. The two Skyhawks overflew the frigate's masts and headed away. A minute behind them, the second pair of Skyhawks headed towards *Coventry*, which was ahead of *Broadsword*. Capt Hart-Dyke turned his ship to starboard, to allow Sea Dart a clear shot, but this also obscured *Broadsword*'s Sea Wolf, which was back in operation.

Coventry's missile passed harmlessly between the two jets, which were now strafing the destroyer as they approached. *Coventry* fought back with her 4.5in guns, Oerlikons and small-arms fire, but it wasn't enough. At 15.24 First Lt Mariano Velasco and Jun Lt Leonardo Barrionuevo dropped three 250kg bombs apiece, before roaring over the ship and heading away towards home. *Coventry* was hit by three bombs on her port side, near the waterline. These carried delayed-action fuses, and they detonated in the destroyer's machinery spaces, causing extensive damage and blowing a hole in the ship's side. *Coventry* began burning and

On 25 May the Type 42 destroyer HMS *Coventry* was struck by three 250kg bombs released by a low-flying A-4B Skyhawk, flown by First Lt Mariano Velasco. When their delay fuses went off, they blew a hole in the ship at the waterline, and created a major fire. *Coventry* capsized and sank 19mins later, taking 19 of her crew down with her.

The arming of Argentinian naval Super Étendard strike aircraft A-204 piloted by Lt Julio Barraza at BAN Río Grande on 25 May. The technicians have just fitted an Exocet anti-ship missile to a pod under the aircraft's starboard wing. That evening the Exocet would be one of two launched at the British Task Force. One of them would strike and cripple the SS *Atlantic Conveyor*.

listing heavily, and Capt Hart-Dyke gave the order to abandon ship. The destroyer sank just 22 minutes later. The attack cost the lives of 19 of her crew. It was a grievous blow to the Task Force, but more setbacks were to come.

While the attack was underway, two Exocet-armed Super Étendards took off from Río Grande, piloted by Capt Roberto Curilovic and Lt Julio Barraza. Their objective was the two British carriers, which were now thought to be in range. The two jets flew towards the north-east, and they refuelled over the sea 185 miles east of Puerto Deseado. They then turned east, flying at sea level, to reach a position about 250 miles to the north-east of the Falklands. Then they turned south, towards the area where intelligence reports suggested the Task Force was operating. This route also meant they should avoid the British CAP screen over the islands. At 16.08, some 15 minutes after sunset, Curilovic began picking up electronic emissions. It was the Task Force. So, the jets turned towards them, flying 50ft over the sea, at 650 knots. Then, at 16.34, they climbed to acquire the British ships on radar.

As they did, they were detected by the air-search radar on the Type 21 frigate HMS *Ambuscade*. The alarm was raised, and on the carriers the decoy Lynx helicopters were sent up. However, it was too late. By then, at 16.38 the Argentinian pilots had already launched their Exocets at a range of 26 miles and had banked away towards the north-west. The ships in the Task Force launched chaff to deflect the missiles, but they were already both sea-skimming towards their target, the container ship *Atlantic Conveyor*. She lacked any form of defence, even chaff. It was probably this cloud of reflective foil launched by *Ambuscade* which had deflected one of the missiles, but the other locked on to the merchantman, and at 16.41 it struck her port quarter.

Although the Exocet didn't explode, the hit caused a huge fire, which slowly engulfed the container ship. Meanwhile, the Task Force fired at other spurious contacts before these were proved to be non-existent. Helicopters were sent to rescue the survivors of *Atlantic Conveyor*, but 12 of her crew were killed, including her master, Capt Ian North. Her cargo of three Chinook, six Wessex and one Lynx helicopter were also destroyed – helicopters which had been earmarked to support the drive on Port Stanley. Now, thanks to the Exocet strike, the British troops would have to march there on foot. The fire also destroyed spare parts, a portable landing and tons of stores earmarked for the land troops, including tents. The *Atlantic Conveyor*, burned-out and abandoned, eventually sank five days later, on 30 May. The Argentinians had demonstrated that, despite heavy losses, they were still a potent force. Now, though, they had used up all but one of their Exocets.

The period from 21 to 25 May had seen major losses on both sides. The Royal Navy had lost two warships, while several others had been damaged, and two Harriers had been lost, because of ground fire. The Argentinians had lost 19 jets during those five days, most of which were felled by Sea Harriers. By 26 May it was clear that the battle of San Carlos had effectively been won by the British. The beachhead was secure, and over 5,000 troops were preparing to advance on Goose Green and Port Stanley. The Argentinian pilots had shown great bravery during their recent attacks, but they had been let down by their ordnance. With so many bombs failing to explode, the superiority of the Sea Harriers amply demonstrated, and with such heavy losses, it was clear to the FAA that this level of offensive was unsustainable. So, operations would be scaled back accordingly.

The endgame

On 26 May the ground troops began their 'yomp' or advance across East Falkland. During the day No. 1 Sqn flew sorties in support, and at 15.10 Sqn Ldr Pook destroyed another Puma near Mount Kent. The Argentinians though, remained inactive, largely due to another cloud front over the coast. The following morning, another Learjet reconnaissance of San Carlos was conducted, but the only attack that resulted was one by a pair of Grupo 5 Skyhawks. First Lt Mariano Velasco and Lt Carlos Osses of 'Poker' flight reached San Carlos Water at

Bomb attack on HMS *Coventry*, 25 May 1982

By 25 May, the landings at San Carlos had almost been completed, despite heavy Argentinian air attacks, and the loss and damage of several warships. So, the Type 42 destroyer HMS *Coventry* with her much-vaunted Sea Dart anti-aircraft missile system was sent to patrol the area to the north of Pebble Island, supported by a 'gatekeeper', the Type 22 frigate HMS *Broadsword*, armed with a highly-effective shorter-range Sea Wolf system. As 25 May was Argentina's National Day, some sort of attack was expected.

Sure enough, two pairs of Argentinian Skyhawks armed with conventional bombs launched attacks against the two ships. Approaching them from over Pebble Island to make detection difficult, the first pair targeted *Broadsword*. They approached her just above sea level, and weren't detected until it was too late. As a result, *Broadsword* was hit by a 1,000lb bomb, which wrecked her helicopter, damaged her flight deck and started a fire. Then, a minute later, the second two Skyhawks appeared.

Capt Hart-Dyke of *Coventry* turned to starboard to give his Sea Dart a clear arc of fire, but, when launched, the missile passed between the two sea-skimming Argentinian jets. The turn also blocked the arc of *Broadsword*'s Sea Wolf. First Lt Mariano Velasco in C-207 was slightly ahead and to the left of Jun Lt Leonardo Barrioneuvo in C-212. Both jets fired their 20mm guns as they approached, and *Coventry*'s crew replied with Oerlikons, small arms and even her 4.5in gun. Then, at 15.23, Velasco climbed sharply and released three 250kg bombs, all of which hit *Coventry* amidships. Moments later Barrioneuvo did the same, but his bombs overshot their target. After roaring over *Coventry*, the two Skyhawks made their escape. The delayed-action bombs detonated, and *Coventry* capsized and sank 22 minutes later. Nineteen of her crew were killed in the attack, and 30 wounded.

The illustration shows the final moment of the attack, as Velasco releases his three bombs. In the background, *Broadsword*, with her missile arcs blocked by *Coventry*, is helpless to intervene.

The Argentinian-built FMA IA-58 Pucará (meaning 'fortress') was a light ground-attack aircraft used by the Fuerza Aérea Argentina during the conflict. This aircraft, of the Grupo 3 de Ataque was deployed at EAN Malvinas (Port Stanley airfield).

16.50, after a 50-minute flight from Río Gallegos. Their target was a stores dump at Ajax Bay, on the inlet's western shore. Two 400kg bombs killed five men there, but Velasco's Skyhawk was hit by 40mm Bofors rounds fired by *Intrepid*, and his jet crashed over West Falkland. Velasco though, ejected safely. The remaining four unexploded bombs that hit the dump were eventually defused.

Meanwhile, while flying in support of the 2 Para advance on Goose Green, Sqn Ldr Bob Iveson and Flt Lt Mark Hare of No. 1 Sqn dropped cluster bombs on Argentinian positions. Iveson was shot down by ground fire, but he ejected successfully. During the night of 27–28 May, the British paratroopers continued their advance, despite harassing attacks by Pucarás, which were discouraged on 28 May when two were shot down by Blowpipe SAMs and small-arms fire. A third Pucará crashed nearby due to the low cloud and mist. The bad weather limited the British pilots too, although Harrier GR3s carried out some rocket strikes around Mount Kent and Goose Green, which greatly demoralized the Goose Green garrison. By this stage, British reinforcements were arriving; 5th Infantry Brigade, made up of the Guard regiments was about to join the land forces, while fresh warships and supply vessels were strengthening the Task Force.

During the two-day battle of Goose Green which followed, more rocket attacks were conducted by No. 1 Sqn, and these proved highly effective. However, that day 801 NAS

This view of HMS *Hermes* clearly shows the bulbous appearance of her 'ski jump' ramp, compared to the slightly more elegant version in HMS *Invincible*. Her lines though, are unmistakably those of a British carrier, which can trace its lineage back to the Royal Navy's armoured carriers of World War II.

The Type 42 destroyer HMS *Exeter* commanded by Capt Hugh Balfour arrived to reinforce the Task Force midway through the campaign. She was a Batch 2 version of the class, with an improved radar fit, and proved her worth, downing three Argentinian aircraft, using her Sea Dart air defence system.

lost another Sea Harrier during an accident during take-off, but the pilot ejected. Less fortunate was Sqn Ldr Pook of No. 1 Sqn the following day, Sunday 30 May, whose Harrier GR3 was hit during ground attacks around Mount Kent. He was hit by ground fire and was forced to eject over the sea, 30 miles from *Hermes*, and was eventually rescued, floating in his inflatable dinghy. This though, coincided with an attack by a Super Étendard on the carrier, using Argentina's last Exocet. Capt Alejandro Francisco's aircraft was accompanied by a second Super Étendard, and four bomb-armed Skyhawks from Grupo 4. He approached the British fleet from the south-east, and at 14.30 Francisco launched his missile. The two Super Étendards then turned for home, while the Skyhawks pressed on, each armed with two 250kg bombs.

The Argentinians thought they were targeting *Invincible*. In fact, their target was the newly arrived Type 42 destroyer *Exeter*, supported by the Type 21 frigate HMS *Avenger*, deployed well ahead of the CVBG. The Exocet launch was detected, and chaff was launched in time, which deflected the missile, and it fell harmlessly into the sea. However, *Avenger* also claimed to have hit it with their 4.5in gun. The four A-4C Skyhawks carried out their attack, but two piloted by Lt José Vázquez and Lt Omar Castillo were both shot down by *Exeter*'s Sea Dart system, and the pilots were killed. The other two Skyhawks, piloted by Lt Ernesto Ureta and Jun Lt Geraldo Isaac both released their bombs, but these narrowly missed their targets. Neither British ship was damaged, although the Argentinians later claimed to have damaged *Invincible*. At the time though, she was 20 miles away to the north-east.

By then, Goose Green had been captured by 2 PARA, and the advance towards Port Stanley was well underway. This meant that while there was still activity in San Carlos Water, with the landing of reinforcements and supplies, the focus of the air campaign became the support of the drive on the island's capital. From 29 May, Canberras were used to fly high-level night-bombing raids on San Carlos and other land-based targets on East Falkland. These created some degree of alarm, but they were largely ineffectual, and on 1 June four only narrowly escaped being ambushed by Sea Harriers. However, the CAP did have some success that Tuesday morning. At 10.50, Lt Cdr 'Sharkey' Ward of 801 NAS shot down a C-130 Hercules with Sidewinders and cannon. The Hercules was being used for radar surveillance, a risky undertaking by the FAA, and one that they wouldn't repeat.

However, at 15.00 that day 801 NAS lost a Sea Harrier south of Port Stanley. Flt Lt Ian Mortimer's jet was brought down by a Roland missile, fired from the airfield, 7 miles away. Mortimer ejected safely though, and was eventually rescued. Meanwhile, No. 1 Sqn's strength was boosted by two GR3s, which had flown south from Ascension Island, supported by Victor refuelling planes. This meant the RAF squadron now had five operational jets.

A C-130 Hercules transport plane of the Argentinian Air Force. These lumbering, vulnerable aircraft made regular supply runs between Comodoro Rivadavia and Río Gallegos air bases on the Argentinian mainland and Port Stanley airfield. The last flight there was on 13 June, the day before the Argentinian surrender.

Poor weather over the next three days limited flying operations, but British helicopters were used to move troops forward, to within 10 miles of Port Stanley. At Port San Carlos the Royal Engineers also managed to complete a makeshift runway using slotted aluminium sheets, ideal for Harriers and helicopters alike.

The poor weather might have hindered local flying operations, but it didn't prevent the *Black Buck* flights. After two cancelled missions in mid- to late May, *Black Buck 5* went ahead on 31 May. This time, instead of Port Stanley airfield, the target was the Argentinian air-search radar station nearby. Two Shrike anti-radiation missiles were launched but missed the target. *Black Buck 7* early on 4 May was a repeat mission, but it proved equally unsuccessful. However, by Saturday 5 June conditions had briefly improved, allowing CAP patrols to be resumed over San Carlos. Now, the airfield, dubbed 'Sid's Strip' could be used for refuelling, which dramatically increased patrol time in the area. However, the weather closed in again, and it was Monday morning before both sides could resume operations.

The Argentinians began by sending up four Learjets, for a high-altitude photo reconnaissance of the islands. However, *Exeter*, patrolling to the north of Falkland Sound, detected one of them over Pebble Island and engaged it with Sea Dart. At 10.17, the Learjet was hit, and its five-man crew died when the aircraft crashed on Pebble Island. This had been a foolhardy enterprise for the FAA, but it needed hard information on British naval dispositions. Now, armed with that information, it was able to plan a series of attacks that proved it was still in the fight, and a determined foe. During the morning of Tuesday 8 May, the British concentration around Port Stanley was gathering pace. To the south-west of Port Stanley, the landing ships *Sir Galahad* and *Sir Tristram* were approaching Bluff Cove near the settlement of Fitzroy. On board were the Welsh Guards, there to reinforce 5th Brigade before the final advance. Meanwhile, in Falkland Sound the old Type 12 frigate HMS *Plymouth* was providing cover for the supply base and airstrip there.

In Río Gallegos, eight Skyhawks from Grupo 4 took off for a strike on British transport ships near Fitzroy and were refuelled soon after take-off. Three A-4s encountered problems refuelling and had to turn back. The remainder though, pressed on towards their target. Meanwhile, six Daggers of Grupo 6 left San Julián, and although one had to return to base, the rest set off towards Fitzroy too, bringing the total size of the two strikes to ten aircraft. They dropped down low well before they reached the Falklands, but visibility was poor, and they passed through a succession of rain squalls. The two groups took different routes. The Skyhawks led by Snr Lt Carlos Cachón approached Fitzroy from the south-west, while the Daggers led by Capt Carlos Rohde flew northwards up Falkland Sound, intending to bank right up Grantham Sound, to approach Fitzroy from the west.

Then, the Daggers spotted Plymouth, and Rohde decided to attack the frigate. On board *Plymouth* Capt David Pentreath saw them approaching at low level. He turned his ship hard to port and called for full speed as his crew opened fire with their Seacats, Oerlikons and small arms. The five Daggers came round and began their approach in line astern, aiming for the frigate's port side, while strafing as they approached. The first bomb struck the frigate's funnel at 14.02, and three other hits followed, all from 1,000lb bombs. The funnel hit was of no real significance, while two more smashed into the Limbo ASW mortar at the frigate's stern before continuing on over the side. The fourth struck the flight deck and rolled over the side, but detonated a depth charge that started a fire and injured five crewmen.

Plymouth had survived, but only just. The Daggers headed home, and while Sea Harriers tried to intercept, the Argentinian jets outran them and made it home safely. Meanwhile, over 40 miles away near Fitzroy, the five Skyhawks sighted the two landing ships, and turned to attack them. Three jets headed for *Galahad*, and two for *Tristram*. With little in the way of incoming fire, the pilots enjoyed a textbook run, and at 14.10 *Sir Galahad* was hit by three bombs. These exploded on the decks of the packed landing ship, which was soon engulfed in flames. It was carnage. Burning soldiers jumped into the water, while others boarded life dinghies. Sea Kings appeared to winch off survivors. By then, 48 people had been killed, and scores more wounded or badly burned. *Sir Tristram* was hit by two bombs, killing two crew, and the ship was badly damaged, but most of her soldiers were relatively unscathed. *Galahad* was burned out, damaged beyond repair. She was scuttled on 21 June.

This attack had taken the British unawares, and unprepared. The CAP was called away to intercept the Daggers, and the landing craft were unescorted. However, the British would have some form of revenge. At 14.30 four Grupo 5 Skyhawks of 'Mazo' flight left Río Gallegos, looking for more landing craft. Over Choiseul Sound two of them, flown by 1st Lt Danilo Bolzán and Jun Lt Alfredo Vázquez spotted a small one, F4 from HMS *Fearless*, en route from Goose Green to Fitzroy. They attacked as dusk fell, and Vázquez bombed and sank it, killing six men. However, the Skyhawks had been spotted by the British CAP, two Sea Harriers of 800 NAS. Flight Lt David Morgan and Lt David Smith were flying at 10,000ft over the Sound when they spotted an aircraft attacking the landing craft. Morgan dived and noticed there were three or four Skyhawks ahead of him, not just one.

He recalled what followed the launch of his first Sidewinder at 16.47: 'My missile did a quick initial junk, and then went off after him and exploded near his tail. There was a huge fireball, and wreckage began to fall into the water.' The two other Skyhawks didn't

The landing ship RFA *Sir Galahad*, pictured ablaze in Bluff Cove, off the south-eastern coast of East Falkland, on 8 June. That afternoon she was bombed by Argentinian Skyhawks and was hit by three bombs. Her consort, RFA *Sir Tristram*, was hit by two more. A total of 48 men were killed in the attack, and in the blaze that followed, most of whom were members of the Welsh Guards. Five died aboard the *Sir Tristram*, making this the heaviest human loss in an air attack of the whole campaign.

Port Stanley airfield (renamed EAM Malvinas by the Argentinians), pictured after extensive bombing by both the aircraft of the CVBG and by RAF Vulcans. These attacks rendered it unsuitable for use by large jet aircraft, although it was still used by light aircraft, and, surprisingly, by C-130 cargo planes until the very end of the conflict.

react, so Morgan locked on with his second missile and fired it, which struck the Skyhawk's wing and brought it down. Then, Smith chased the remaining two Skyhawks, and when Morgan climbed out of the way he launched one, which brought down a third Skyhawk, just a few feet above the water. As Smith put it later, 'He must have been flying so low that the missile impact and ground impact seemed almost instantaneous.' All three Argentinian pilots were killed.

Another flight of Skyhawks was in the area too. Four of them from Grupo 4 had taken off from San Julián at 15.00, to carry out a ground attack on British positions around Fitzroy. They arrived over the area at around 17.00, a little after dark. They were guided by the burning hull of *Galahad*. This time, though, they came under heavy ground fire, and were engaged by Rapier SAM batteries. All four jets were hit, but they dropped their bombs and managed to limp home. Meanwhile, two other CAP Sea Harriers from 801 NAS had spotted contrails at around 35,000ft above West Falkland. These were Mirages of Grupo 8, there to help provide cover for the returning Skyhawks. They soon turned away though, as the surviving Skyhawks also made for home. It had been a dramatic day, and the Argentinians had inflicted the largest number of casualties the British Army had suffered on a single day since World War II. However, the FAA had also taken a mauling, leaving it increasingly short of operational fighter-bombers.

The next few days were something of a reprieve for the British. While bad weather over Argentina grounded the FAA's aircraft, the skies were clear over the Falklands. So, not only were CAP missions flown, but No. 1 Sqn also launched a series of ground-attack strikes on Argentinian positions around Port Stanley, as well as photo-reconnaissance flights over the Argentinian defences. Meanwhile, every available helicopter was used to move forward troops and stores for the final drive on Port Stanley. By 11 June, as the FAA remained grounded, Sea Harriers were taken off CAP missions to join in the ground-attack strikes. Early that morning 800 NAS carried out a 'toss-bombing' strike on the airfield, using radar-fused air-burst bombs, released 4 miles from the target. These proved successful, as fires were seen burning there for several hours. Despite heavy ground fire, all of the planes made it back.

Meanwhile, the military offensive was gathering pace. On the night of 11–12 June, the British assaulted the high ground to the west of Port Stanley. While 42 Cdo captured Mount Harriet, and 45 Cdo took Two Sisters, 3 PARA had a tougher time of it on Mount Longdon. By dawn on Saturday morning though, with these peaks in British hands, the airfield was within range of British guns, and the fate of the Argentinian garrison was sealed. Still, the ground fighting continued, and two nights later 2 PARA had to assault Wireless Ridge, while the 2nd Scots Guards did the same in a more costly attack on Tumbledown Mountain. This, then, placed the British within 3 miles of Port Stanley. By Monday morning, as Argentinian troops fled back through the town, it was clear that the defences had crumbled, and the battle had been won.

During these climactic few days, aircraft from the CVBG continued to support the ground offensive with low-level strikes, while the CAP missions continued over the Falklands. On one of the last flights into Port Stanley airfield, a C-130 had unloaded an Exocet launching cell, taken from an Argentinian warship. It was mounted on a truck, and early on 12 June it was fired at Glamorgan, which was close inshore, carrying out a naval bombardment mission. The destroyer was hit and badly damaged, even though the missile didn't explode. That same night a final *Black Buck* mission was launched from Ascension, and while its aim was to degrade the airfield's defences, the bombing proved only marginally effective.

They overflew the airfield, before turning round to the east, to bomb British positions around Mount Kent and Mount Longdon. They were met by heavy anti-aircraft fire, but they all released their bombs. However, the soft peaty ground absorbed most of the blasts, and apart from two helicopters being damaged, little else was achieved, and there were no casualties, although an airborne Sea King helicopter had a narrow escape.

The last act of the air campaign came that evening when Grupo 2's Canberras returned for a nocturnal bombing raid. As usual no real damage was done, but this time, on the return flight, they were tracked by *Exeter*. The destroyer launched a Sea Dart, which struck Capt Roberto Pastran's Canberra, shortly after dropping its bombs over Mount Kent. He ejected, but his navigator didn't and died in the crash. Pastran landed in the sea, and later he and his dinghy drifted ashore on the northern coast of West Falkland. It was the last plane shot down during the conflict.

Dawn on Monday 14 June brought a renewal of shelling by both sides, but the weather conditions prevented any air strikes. It cleared at noon though, and two Harrier GR3s were deployed, to launch laser-guided bombs at the airfield's defences. Then, at 12.25, as they approached their target, the strike was called off. The Harriers flew in a holding pattern, but some 15 minutes later the air liaison officer radioed them and explained the reason: 'The people on the target you were going for have already given in – and there's a white flag over Stanley!' It was all over. The Argentinians had surrendered, and the Falklands had been liberated. In the CVBG there was no immediate celebration, as they still thought an attack might come from Argentina itself. It never did, and the ceasefire that followed the garrison's surrender led to a peace that has lasted ever since. The air campaign was now officially over. The two carriers could now return to Portsmouth, where they and their crews would enjoy a memorable homecoming and be rightly feted as the true heroes of the conflict.

Alferez ('Pilot Officer') Alfredo Alberto Vázquez was one of two A-4B Skyhawk pilots of Grupo 5's 'Mazo' flight who were shot down over Choiseul Sound in East Falkland during the afternoon of 8 June, by a Sea Harrier FRS.1s piloted by Flt Lt David Morgan of 800 NAS. Morgan's wingman, Lt David Smith, then shot down the third Skyhawk from 'Mazo' flight.

ANALYSIS AND CONCLUSION

A symbol of victory – a Sea Harrier of 801 NAS pictured flying over the capital of the Falkland Islands, Port Stanley, shortly after the ceasefire. For most of those involved in the air campaign, the real reward was the immense delight felt by the islanders following their liberation from Argentinian occupation.

The air campaign fought over the South Atlantic was never officially part of a 'war'. Instead, it was dubbed a 'conflict'. For those who took part, though, it was a bona fide war in every sense. While the Argentinians were able to operate from established airfields, the Royal Navy had to operate from two relatively small carriers. The fighting was characterized by several other unusual factors. These included the geographical constraints of the distance between Argentina and the Falklands, and the radius of action of the British Harriers. Both imposed limits on flying time in the operational area. So, the Argentinians used mid-air refuelling to reach the archipelago, while for the British Task Force Cdr, the positioning of his CVBG would be crucial to the effectiveness of his Sea Harriers over the islands. The campaign saw the first combat use of a Sea Harrier, and it proved a war-winning aircraft. It also saw the deployment of sea-skimming Exocet anti-ship missiles, and these too proved their effectiveness.

The air campaign could be divided into several stages. It began in earnest on 1 May, when the British CVBG came within strike range of the Falklands. This first day of air combat demonstrated the effectiveness of both the Sea Harrier and its improved Sidewinder missiles. This was followed by a period when both sides vied for control of the air and seas around the islands. During this phase the key British aim was the safeguarding of the CVBG. This period saw the first successful deployment of Exocet. Then, on 21 May, the focus for both sides shifted to San Carlos Water. Then, once the British bridgehead was established, focus changed again, to the support of the ground troops, and their resupply. This then, saw the operational centre of gravity shift towards Port Stanley.

Some elements stand out from the air campaign. There were six days in all when the air operations were particularly intensive. Five of these were between 21 and 25 May. This was when the Argentinians increased their attacks in an attempt to prevent the British from securely establishing themselves ashore. They flew 180 sorties over those five days, and 117 over the Falklands. During these sorties, they lost 19 Daggers and Skyhawks, the majority at the hands of Sea Harriers. This represented one aircraft in six of those entering the combat area. In this same period, British Harriers flew 300

CAP and ground-attack sorties, a remarkable achievement for the pilots and support staff aboard the two carriers.

Morale was very high among the British pilots throughout the air campaign. It had been among the Argentinian pilots too, and anti-ship attacks were pressed home with commendable courage. Losses though, led to a diminution in resolve by the FAA, and a reluctance to press home attacks in the face of the British CAP. British naval losses were significant, whether from conventional bombing or Exocet. From the Argentinian perspective the success of the Exocet-armed Super Étendards was one of the highlights of the campaign. These aircraft scored two hits with their five Exocets, resulting in the crippling of both *Sheffield* and *Atlantic Conveyor*.

Less successful was the use of conventional ordnance. Many Argentinian bombs failed to explode, something that saved the British from greater losses. They did, though, cripple or sink *Coventry*, *Ardent*, *Antelope* and *Sir Galahad*. Several other British warships were badly damaged. Despite the courage shown by the Argentinian pilots, they were poorly served by their faulty ordnance. An unsung Argentinian success was the use of transport aircraft, including the C-130 Hercules, to reinforce and supply the Falkland garrison. This showed that, ultimately, the RAF *Black Buck* strikes had failed to put Port Stanley airfield out of action.

To be fair, the same could be said for the ground-attack strikes by Sea Harriers and Harrier GR3s. Few of these attacks caused any significant damage, and the deployment of a specialist ground-attack formation failed to provide the results British commanders wished for. Still, these ground-attack missions played a major part in demoralizing the Argentinian garrison, particularly during the closing stages of the campaign. This alone made these operations worthwhile.

The real star though, was the Sea Harrier. Its high success rate in air-to-air combat made it the stand-out aircraft of the campaign. In the hands of the experienced Fleet Air Arm and RAF pilots on 800 and 801 NAS, these aircraft came to dominate the skies over the Falklands. In all, 22 Argentinian aircraft were shot down by Sea Harriers, 18 of these using Sidewinders. These 'kills' included nine Daggers, seven Skyhawks, two Mirages, two Pucarás, a Canberra and a Hercules. Another four aircraft were destroyed by Harrier GR3s on the ground. By contrast, the British lost six Sea Harriers and four GR3s to ground fire or accidents. Of these, all but one of the Sea Harriers were lost in operational accidents, and all but one of the GR3s to ground fire.

The outstanding fact from all this is that no Sea Harriers were shot down in air-to-air combat, a statistic the Fleet Air Arm put down to a mixture of the improved Sidewinder and a greatly superior standard of pilot training compared to their Argentinian counterparts. Certainly, after the conflict, both sides released statistics or claims which have proved unreliable, either in part or in their totality, such as the damage to a British carrier by the Argentinians, or a hugely inflated total of claimed 'kills' by British weapons systems during the attacks over San Carlos Water.

By now, with over four decades of detailed research, a clear picture can emerge – one where the British were well served by the Sea Harrier, and by their superbly trained pilots, while the Argentinians displayed immense courage, despite their lower standard of training and often faulty ordnance. The real heroes of this campaign, then, are the pilots of both sides, who put their lives on the line for their country, and for what they believed.

The rust-streaked but victorious flagship of the British Task Force, HMS *Hermes*, pictured in the English Channel on the day before her triumphal return to Portsmouth. In the background is the brand new Invincible-class carrier HMS *Illustrious*, commanded by Capt Jock Slater, which would replace the *Hermes* and *Invincible* on patrol off the Falklands.

FURTHER READING

Beaver, Paul, *Encyclopaedia of the Fleet Air Arm since 1945*, Patrick Stephens Ltd, Wellingborough: 1987

Beaver, Paul, *The British Aircraft Carrier*, Patrick Stephens Ltd, Wellingborough: 1987

Brown, Davis, *The Royal Navy and the Falklands War*, Leo Cooper Ltd, London: 1987

Burden, Rodney; Draper, Michael; Rough, Douglas; Smith, Colin and Wilton, David, *Falklands: The Air War*, Arms & Armour Press, London: 1986

Childs, Nick, *The Age of Invincible: The Ship that Defined the Modern Royal Navy*, Pen & Sword, Barnsley: 2009

Drought, Charles, *NP.1840: The Loss of Atlantic Conveyor*, Countyvise Ltd, Birkenhead: 2003

Ethell, Jeffrey and Price, Alfred, *Air War South Atlantic*, Sidgwick and Jackson, London: 1983

Freedman, Lawrence, *The Official History of the Falklands Campaign Vol. 2*, Routledge, London: 2007

Friedman, Norman, *Naval Radar*, Conway Maritime Press, London: 1981

Friedman, Norman, *British Destroyers & Frigates: The Second World War and After*, Seaforth Publishing, Barnsley: 2006

Gardiner, Robert (ed.), *Conway's All the World's Fighting Ships, 1947–1982 Part I: The Western Powers*, Conway Maritime Press, London: 1983

Hart-Dyke, David, *Four Weeks in May: A Captain's Story of War at Sea*, Atlantic Books, London: 2007

Hobbs, David, *British Aircraft Carriers: Design, Development and Service Histories*, Seaforth Publishing, Barnsley: 2013

Hobbs, David, *The British Carrier Strike Fleet after 1945*, Seaforth Publishing, Barnsley: 2015

Hobson, Chris and Noble, Andrew, *Falklands Air War*, Midlands Publishing, Hinckley: 2002

Morgan, David, *Hostile Skies: The Battle for the Falklands*, Weidenfeld & Nicolson, London: 2006

Sandham-Bailey, Chris, *Sea Harriers of the Falklands War*, Mortons Media Group, Horncastle: 2022

Shields, John, *Air Power in the Falklands Conflict: An Operational Insight into Air Warfare in the South Atlantic*, Air World, Barnsley: 2021

Smith, Gordon, *Battles of the Falklands War*, Ian Allen Ltd, London: 1989

Ward, Cdr 'Sharkey', *Sea Harrier over the Falklands: A Maverick at War*, Leo Cooper, Barnsley: 1992

White, Rowland, *Harrier 809: Britain's Legendary Jump Jet and the Untold Story of the Falklands War*, Bantam Books, London: 2020

Woodward, Admiral Sandy, *One Hundred Days: The Memoirs of the Falklands Battle Group Commander*, Harper Collins, London: 1992

INDEX

References to images are in **bold**.

Admiralty 4, 13
air bases: map **10**
Air Defence Command (CAD) 8
air-to-air missiles (AAM) 16, **19**, **26**
aircraft, Argentine 8, 9, 11–12, 15–16
    Dagger **24**
    Neptune 42
aircraft, British 27, 30
    Harrier GR3s 4, 5, **7**, 16
    see also Sea Harriers
Alacrity, HMS 31, 33, 37
Alférez Sobral, ARA 41
Ambuscade, HMS 82
amphibious landings 25, 27; *see also* San Carlos Water
Anaya, Adm Jorge 22, 24
Antelope, HMS 9, 31, **65**, **66**
    and attack 76, 77, 93
Antrim, HMS 31–32, 33, 55
    and missile air defence **18**, 19
    and San Carlos Water 58, 65, 66–67, 68, 74
ARA *see* Argentine Navy (ARA)
Arca, Lt Jose 74
Ardent, HMS 11, 55, 58, 59, 93
    and missile air defence **18**, 19
    and San Carlos Water 68, 69, 72–73, 74
Ardiles, Lt José 40
Argentina 22–25, 27, 78, 80, 91
Argentine Air Force (FAA) 4, 8–9, 25, 27, **36**
    and order of battle 28–29
    and sorties 92
    see also aircraft, Argentine
Argentine Army (EA) 9
Argentine Navy (ARA) 8, 9, 11, 25, 27
    and air attack **78–79**, 80
Argonaut, HMS 19, 55
    and San Carlos Water 58, 64, 66, 71–72, 74
Ark Royal, HMS 17
Arrarás, Lt Juan 51
Arrow, HMS 33, 37, 45
Ascension Island 30, 32
Atlantic Conveyor, SS 11, 47, 53, 54–55, **77**
    and attack 82–83, 93
attrition 40–43, 45–47, 50–56
Auld, Lt Cdr Andy 34, 53, 76, 77, 80
Avenger, HMS 87

Bahía Buen Suceso, ARA 53
Bahia Paraiso, ARA 23
Baigorri, Capt Alberto 40
Ball, Flt Lt Ted 42
Barker, Capt Nick 23
Barraza, Lt Julio 82
Barrionuevo, Jun Lt Leonardo 81, 83

Barton, Flt Lt Paul 35–37
Batt, Lt Cdr Gordon 'Gordy' 42, 47, 53, 77
Bean, Lt Pedro 66
Bedacarratz, Capt Augusto 42, 43, 47
Benitez, Capt Jorge 59
Bernhardt, Lt Juan 71
Black, Capt Jeremy 13, **29**
Blissett, Lt Cdr Mike 34–35, 70–71
Bolzán, Lt Danilo 89
bombs 12, **36**, 66–67, 93
    and 'toss-bombing' 52, 53
Bonzo, Capt Hector 41
Braithwaite, Lt Cdr Dave 76
Brilliant, HMS 32, 33, 50–52
    and missile air defence **18**, 19
    and San Carlos Water 58, 68, 71, 73–74
Britain *see* Great Britain
British Antarctic Survey (BAS) 23
Broadsword, HMS 31, 33, 47, 77, 80
    and attack **76**, 81, 83
    and San Carlos Water 58, 66, 67, 74
Broadwater, Cdr Mike 40
Bustos, 1/Lt Oscar 50

Cachón, Snr Lt Carlos 88
CAD *see* Air Defence Command (CAD)
CAE *see* Strategic Air Command (CAE)
Canberra, HMS 31
Carballo, Capt Marcus 81
Carballo, Capt Pablo 69
Cardiff, HMS 51
Carmona, Jr Lt Leonardo 69
Carrier Battle Group (CVBG) 4, 8, 13, 17, 21, 27, 30
Casco, Lt Jorge 47
Castillo, Lt Carlos 65, 80
Castillo, Lt Omar 87
Chile 8, 55
Cimatti, Capt Amilcar 71
Clapp, Cmdre Michael 21
COAN (*Comando de la Aviación Naval Argentina*) 9, 12
Colombo, Capt Jorge 41
Comodoro Somellera, ARA 41
Conqueror (submarine) 31, 32, 41
Conqueror, HMS 35
Coventry, HMS 9, 32, 33, 43, **75**
    and attack 47, 81–82, 83, **84–85**, 93
    and gatekeeping 77, 80
Craig, Lt Cdr Alisdair 68
Crespo, Brig Ernesto 9, **11**, 25
Crippa, Lt Guillermo 61, 64
Cuerva, Capt Garcia 37, 38
Curilovic, Capt Roberto 82
Curtis, Lt Alan 40, 46

Dellepiane, Jun Lt Alferez 51
Diaz, Capt Rául 80

Dimeglio, Capt Norberto 65
dogfights 5, 37, **38–39**, 40
    and San Carlos Water 73–74
    and West Falkland 61, **62–63**
Donadille, Capt Guillermo 61, 73
Dozo, Brig Lami 8–9, 22
Dunnose Head 75–76

East Falkland 22, 24, 25, 34, 54; *see also* San Carlos Water
Endurance, HMS 23, 32
Exeter, HMS 19, 87, 88, 91
Exocet missiles 41, 82–83, 92
    and HMS *Sheffield* 43, **44**, 45, 47, **48–50**
Eyton-Jones, Lt Cdr John 35–36, 46

FAA *see* Argentine Air Force (FAA)
Falkland Sound 64–66
Falklands Islands 4, 22–25, 27
    map **14**
    see also Port Stanley; San Carlos Water
Falklands Military Garrison (*Guarnición Militar Malvinas*) 9, 25, 68–69
Farias, Lt Jorge 47
FAS *see* Southern Air Force (FAS)
Fearless, HMS 31, 59
Fieldhouse, Adm Sir John 21, 31
Fort Austin, RFA 55, 67, 80
France 11, 22
Francisco, Capt Alejandro 87
Frederiksen, Lt Cdr 'Fred' 35, 75, 68, 71

Galtieri, Leopoldo 8, 22, 24
Garcia, Capt Jorge 80
Gavazzi, Lt Fausto 51
Gedge, Lt Cdr Tim 76
General Belgrano, ARA 30, 33, 40–41
George, Lt Andy 71
Glamorgan, HMS **25**, 31–32, 33, 37, 38
    and East Falkland 54
    and Pebble Island 52
Glasgow, HMS 32, 33, 43,, 50–52, **72**
    and missile air defence **18**, 19
Glover, Flt Lt Jeff 60
González, Capt Horacio 71
Goose Green 34, 35, **38–39**, 64–65
    and attacks 42, 45
    and battle 86–87
Grantham Sound 58
Great Britain 22–23, 24–25, 27, 30
Grytviken 23, 24, 32
Guadagnini, Lt Luciano 76
Guerrico, ARA 24

Hale, Lt Ian 75
Hale, Lt Martin 37, 40, 68, 76
Hare, Flt Lt Mark 60, 86
Hargreaves, Lt Simon 53

INDEX

Hart-Dyke, Capt David 81, 82, 83
Hercules, ARA 40
Hermes, HMS 4, 13, 15, 17, 19, 21, **27**
 and attrition 42–43
 and *Black Buck* 34–35
 and departure 31
 and return **93**
 and San Carlos Water 59, 60
 and Sea Harriers **41**, **53**, **54**

Illustrious, HMS **93**
Intrepid, HMS 59, 86
Invincible, HMS 4, 13, 15, 17, 19, 21, **28**
 and attrition 42–43
 and departure 32
 and *Mikado* operation 55
 and San Carlos Water 59
 and Sea Harriers **70**
Isaac, Jun Lt Geraldo 87
Iveson, Sqn Ldr Bob 55, 86

Janett, Capt Roberto 66, 67

Layman, Capt Kit 71
Leach, Adm Sir Henry 21
Leeming, Flt Lt John 74
Lombardo, Vice Adm Juan 9, **21**, 27, 40
Lopez, Lt Nestor 71
Lucero, Lt Ricardo 80
Luna, 1/Lt Hector 71

McHarg, Lt Andy 53
Malvinas *see* Falkland Islands
maps **57**
 air bases **10**
 Falkland Islands **14**
Maritime Exclusion Zone (MEZ) 30
Marquez, Lt Marcello 74
Martinez, Maj Carlos 65, 66
Mayora, Lt Armando 42, 43, 47
Menéndez, Maj Gen Mario 24, 25
Micheloud, 1/Lt Juan 68, 69
Middleton, Capt Linley 13
missile air defence **18**, 19–21
Morell, Lt Clive 'Spaghetti' 74
Moreno, Capt Carlos 66
Morgan, Flt Lt David 17, 35, 47, 76, 89–90
Morgan, Sub-Lt Peter 72
Mortimer, Flt Lt Ian 87

Narwhal, ARA 47
Nivoli, Lt Mario 50
North, Capt Ian 83
nuclear submarines 30

Ogilvy, Lt Cdr Tony 34
Olmeda, RFA 31, 33
operations:
 Black Buck (1982) 33–37, **38–39**, 40, 42, 88, 91
 Corporate (1982) 13
 Mikado (1982) 55
 Rosario (1982) 23–25, 27
 Spring Train (1982) 31
 Sutton (1982) 4, 19, 55–56
Osses, Lt Carlos 83, 86

Palaver, Capt Hugo 80
Pastran, Capt Roberto 91
Patagonia 9
Pebble Island 52, 59–60, 71, 77, 80–81, 88
Penfold, Flt Lt Bertie 35, 37, 40
Pentreath, Capt David 89
Perona, Lt Carlos 37, 38
Philippi, Capt Alberto 74, 76
pilots 12, 15, **36**
Piuma, Maj Gustavo 61
Plymouth, HMS 32, 33, 55, 88, 89
 and San Carlos Water 58, 59
Pook, Sqn Ldr Jerry 55, 60, 75, 87
Port Stanley 4, 87–91
 and *Black Buck* 33–37, **38–39**, 40
Portsmouth Naval Dockyard 31
Proni, Capt Ernesto 42
Puga, Maj Luis 80

Queen Elizabeth 2, SS 53

radar 12, 43
reconnaissance 46–47, 52, 53, 60, 61
Reeve, Sqn Ldr John 42
refuelling 12
Resource, RFA 33
Rinke, Lt Carlos 81
Río Carcaraña, ARA 53, 69
Río Iguazu, ARA 75
Robles, Capt Higinio 71
Rohde, Capt Carlos 66, 88–89
Royal Air Force (RAF) 4, 30, 92–93
 and 1 May dogfight 33–37, **38–39**, 40
 and attrition 40–43, 45–47, 50–56
 see also aircraft, British
Royal Air Force (units):
 800 NAS 13, 15
 801 NAS 13, 15, **37**, **38–39**, 86–87
 809 NAS 54–55
 846 NAS 55
 8012 NAS **31**
Royal Marines 24
Royal Navy (RN) 16, 17, 29, 31–33
 and missile air defence **18**, 19

Salt, Capt Sam 45
San Carlos Water 4–5, 12, 54, 58–61, **62–63**, 64–74
 and preparations 55–56
San Luis (submarine) 35
Sanders, Cdr Jeremy **25**
Santa Fe (submarine) 32
Santísima Trinidad, ARA 40
SAS *see* Special Air Service (SAS)
Sea Cat 19–20
Sea Dart 19, 20
Sea Harriers 4–5, 13, 15–17, 30
 and armament **46**
 and repainting 32
 and success rate 92, 93
Sea Kings 4
Sheffield, HMS 11, 21, **42**
 and departure 32, 33
 and Exocet missile 43, **44**, 45, 47, **48–50**, 93
Sir Belvedere, RFA **61**, 80

Sir Galahad, HMS 9, 80, 88
 and attack 89, 93
Sir Lancelot, RFA 80
Sir Tristram, HMS 88, 89
Smith, Lt Dave 77, 80, 89–90
South Atlantic Military Theatre (*Teatro Operaciones Atlántico Sur*) 9, 25
South Georgia 23–24, 32, 33, 47
South Sandwich Islands 23
Southern Air Force (FAS) 9, 25
Soviet Union 31
Spain 22
Spartan (submarine) 31, 32
Special Air Service (SAS) 32, 52, 58–59, 60
Splendid (submarine) 31, 32
Squire, Wing Cdr Peter 55
Strategic Air Command (CAE) 8–9
Stromness, RFA 31

Taylor, Lt Nick 42
Thatcher, Margaret 21
Thomas, Lt Cdr Neil 70–71
Thomas, Lt Steve 36–37, 38, 61, 68, 73–74
Thule Island 23
Tidespring, RFA 32, 33
Tierra del Fuego 55
Tobin, Cdr Nick 77
Tomba, Sn Lt (Maj) Carlos 68–69
Total Exclusion Zone (TEZ) 30

United Nations (UN) 4, 23, 55
United States of America (USA) 8
Ureta, Lt Ernesto 87

Vázquez, Jun Lt Alfredo 89, **91**
Vázquez, Jun Lt Jorge 50
Vázquez, Lt José 87
Veinticinco de Mayo, ARA 9, 17, 24, 33, **35**
 and Skyhawks **51**
 and strikes 40
Velasco, 1/Lt Mariano 81, 83, 86
Volponi, Lt Héctor 66, 76

Walrus (submarine) 55
Ward, Cdr 'Sharkey' 36, **37**, **65**
 and San Carlos Water 68, 73–74
 and West Falkland 61, **62–63**
Watson, Lt Mike 36
weather conditions 46–47, 52
West, Cdr Alan 59, 68
Woodward, R Adm Sandy 4, 21, **25**, 33
 and ARA attack 80
 and *Black Buck* 34
 and Carrier Battle Group 27, 30
 and HMS *Sheffield* 45
 and San Carlos Water 55
 and SS *Atlantic Conveyor* 54
Wreford-Brown, Cdr Chris 41

Yarmouth, HMS 31, 33, 45, 47, 58
Young, Capt Brian 67

Zelaya, Capt Antonio 51
Zini, Lt Cdr Ruben 81
Zubizarreta, Lt Cdr Carlos 76